QUEEN
of the
DERBY PUB

QUEEN of the DERBY PUB

Kathryn Smick

CREATIVE ARTS BOOK COMPANY
Berkeley ⊕ California

Queen of the Derby Pub is published by Donald S. Ellis
and distributed by Creative Arts Book Company

For information contact:
Creative Arts Book Company
833 Bancroft Way
Berkeley, California 94710
1-800-848-7789

ISBN 0-88739-389-6
Library of Congress Catalog Number 2001097460

Printed in the United States of America

To Ella Thorp Ellis,
writer, teacher, friend

QUEEN
of the
DERBY PUB

- Chapter 1 -

"Hello . . . Hello?"

I was about to hang up on the silence at the other end of the phone when I heard a sniffle and the crumpling of paper. "Helen?" Telephone communication with my sister had been impossible since her surgery for throat cancer. Speechless, she now "talked" with a writing pad and gestures. She had gleaned from a tapping code only the elementary three taps for Yes, two for No. Groping for a question that she could answer I blurted out, "Is something wrong?" I was answered by a jumble of taps. "Helen, I'll come down. I can make it in an hour. Will you be all right until I get there?" Three steady taps reassured me.

Helen had called before, but only with a friend beside her to convey her message. I was puzzled and uneasy as I hurriedly cleared the dinner table. I grabbed a sweatshirt—it would be cool later—and headed for the carport.

Commute travel had already thinned out as my Fiat nosed south on the unbroken ribbon of freeway. The lowering sun cast a glow on the lush green hills where vineyards criss-crossed in patterns that shifted with my passing. At another time I might have been enchanted by the California landscape, but tonight my thoughts, a mix of anxiety and reflection, stayed with Helen. Our sister relationship had never been easy. In our childhood Helen had been a cute little show-off, while I, the older sister, read books and embroidered doilies. In adolescence her no-care, hop-and-skip attitude was a contrast to my penchant for study. After high school we went our separate ways: Helen into a colorful and chaotic life, I into the respectable career of a physician. For most of our lives we were out of touch with each other. Now in our middle years Helen's life-threatening illness ended our estrangement. Glancing at the speedometer I relaxed my foot on the accelerator. When at last a freeway sign announced SAN JOSE it was already dark.

I searched impatiently for Helen's house among the many little look-alike duplexes that lined the long blocks in the northeast part of the city. Helen's place was not easy to find. When I spotted the Derby with its neon-lighted martini glass I knew that it was only half a block away. I slowed to find the house number, then parked in front of the unlit building.

Feeling my way up the concrete steps I reached the porch and opened the unlocked door. "I'm here, Helen," I called, trying to conceal my apprehension. Groping through the small cluttered kitchen I came to the bedroom-living room and reached for the light switch on the wall. Helen lay on the couch on a rumpled gray sheet, naked except for underpants. She blinked with the sudden light, raised her head and motioned me to sit down. Her fair face was streaked with crying; her auburn hair, gray at the temples, was matted from tears and tossing. A roll of skin rested like a limp penis above her right breast—the creation of a plastic surgeon. He had peeled it from her thigh and attached it there within reach of her neck until it would later be grafted onto the cancerous defect. She breathed not through her nose or mouth but directly into the windpipe through a surgical opening in her neck. I had never seen her in such despair. Yet, beneath the drastic physical changes were hints of Helen's past beauty: in her unblemished skin, in her head, held like a ballerina's, on her slender neck.

I pulled a chair near the couch. "I worried about you all the way down here. I couldn't imagine what was wrong."

Listless eyes met mine.

"What happened? What's going on?"

Since her loss of speech Helen's body had developed a compensating language that often projected more than the voice it had replaced. Her blue eyes struggled for expression. Now she soundlessly mouthed words that I couldn't decipher. Frustrated, she waved her hands suggesting disgust with my ineptitude.

"Helen, your recovery's been better than the doctors expected. You're a heroine to all your friends." Then, glancing at the piles of medical supplies in her bathroom, I added, "And you've figured out how to get what you need from the county."

I thought, I'm talking like a doctor, and that's not what she needs right now. But I noticed that my recognition of her achievements brought an appreciative tilt to her chin.

With a struggle she sat up and turned on the lamp at the head of the couch. In the brighter light I saw the small room as I remembered it from an earlier visit: the floor with its dusty brown carpeting, paint peeling from the ceiling, and the framed image of a dancer in a tutu above the dresser. On the bedside table were medicine bottles labeled Miltown, Phenobarbital, Elavil, Seconal and a half-smoked cigarette in a small glass ash tray.

"Why don't you come home with me tonight? I'll bring you back as soon as you feel better."

Helen nodded and began to get up, only to fall back onto the bed. I was in no hurry. I helped her into a bathrobe and then made a pot of tea. She began to brighten as she pulled a comb through her hair and washed her face with a warm washcloth I brought from the bathroom. She picked up the notepad and wrote of the speech clinic and the frustrations of learning to talk with an electronic larynx, of what she'd been eating now that the stomach tube was out, and of her hopes for plastic surgery.

"It all sounds terribly difficult, but you can do it, Helen."

"My doctor says I've done well," she mouthed, without conviction.

We sat in silence as I drank tea and urged Helen to drink hers. Ignoring the tea, she picked up her pencil and pad. "Tom had a heart attack. He's in the ICU." She adjusted the paper for me to read. "I wouldn't have bothered you tonight if he'd been around."

"Why didn't you tell me in the first place, instead of letting me wonder what the hell was going on?" I sounded impatient, too harsh. "Is he going to be OK?"

Helen looked forlorn for an instant, then angrily wrote, "What galls me is that his wife is the only one allowed to visit him." She opened both hands and shrugged.

"Be thankful that his wife wasn't in the way until now," I chided.

Her chin quivered as she wrote, "He was always here for me—whenever I needed him." She dabbed at a tear as it slid onto her cheek. I put my arm around her shoulder.

After a moment of resignation she indicated her intention to dress and walked steadily to the bathroom. She washed her face meticulously, massaged cream and color into her skin, and sprayed Jean Nate onto her armpits.

Then she opened the door of the wardrobe closet. Before the full length mirror on the door she held up one attractive outfit after another and considered each critically. Finally she chose an egg-shell pant suit with a tangerine colored scarf. She pulled a strawberry blond hair piece over her scraggly hair and arranged the chiffon scarf to conceal the white gauze dressing around her neck. Exactly the right makeup completed the transformation. Her eyes shone with satisfaction; her lips smacked approval as she made some minor adjustments before the mirror. Then she packed a few clothes into a suitcase and indicated her readiness to leave.

Suddenly she pivoted, raised her hand in a quick gesture of recollection, and pulled the writing pad from her purse. "I've got to stop at the Derby."

"I'll wait for you in the car."

In front of the Derby she made a pleading motion for me to join her.

"Wouldn't I look silly going in there in these old slacks and sweat shirt? On a Friday night? No, really, I don't mind waiting."

Helen's appearance of hurt and rejection gave way to an angry set of her jaw. She was determined that we should have a drink at the Derby before starting home.

Suddenly I was back in the past of our girlhood, being manipulated, tricked. My solution at that time was to detach myself, leaving her to the companionship of our younger sister Betty. Now it was different. I was dealing with a woman, cagey but ill, perhaps mortally ill. I could not deny her an appearance at the Derby.

As we entered every patron turned to look. Her head held high, her eyes triumphant, Helen swept toward the bar.

She pulled me first to Joe. "My little sister," she wrote proudly.

I suspected that I was no stranger to Helen's friends. She had probably exploited my status as a physician to the fullest.

She continued writing as Joe, beaming admiration, bragged, "I've been drinking with Helen at this bar for fifteen years. She's a good woman."

I read her note to Joe. "Remember last New Years when you had that hangover? I told you my little sister could pull you out of it if she was here."

"Joe, she misleads you with that little sister stuff. She may be an inch taller than I am, but I'm two years older." I lowered my voice to add, "Which makes me all of fifty-two."

Helen motioned me on to Joanie and Shortie who lived just around the corner. Then to Carrie whose husband and seven children were at home while she got away for a few drinks "to keep from blowing a fuse. God, if it weren't for the Derby I'd have cracked up long ago."

The Colonel, white-haired and ruddy faced, boasted that he'd lived in the neighborhood for twenty-five years and hadn't missed a day at the Derby. As we ordered drinks others gathered around us. "You must be Helen's sister; you look alike."

A cocky young man standing apart winked and beckoned to Helen. She sidled up to him, listened attentively to catch his words above the tavern din, then suddenly backed off scowling. He grabbed her by the arm; she lashed back. Then, in apparent response to something he said, she looked incredulous for a moment before she threw her head back, laughed, and punched him playfully.

Sad-faced Carlos, sitting alone at a table, caught her eye and motioned her to cool it. She shrugged indifference, paused, then blew him a kiss.

She turned to greet a new arrival. Carrying a drink and sipping through a straw, she circulated among the Friday night crowd, mouthing greetings, gesticulating, and from time to time pulling out her notepad for a quick message.

Helen's metamorphosis in the last two hours made me feel unneeded. Yet I had committed myself to taking her home with me. I sipped ginger ale and waited, bored and impatient, and grateful that the Derby was ignoring me. It was eleven o'clock, already late for me, when Helen pulled the last of her Creme de Cacao through a straw, put her glass on the counter, and waved a circle of good-byes announcing our departure.

But her proclivity for drama had not yet played itself out on this night.

- Chapter 2 -

On the freeway I relaxed to the engine's purr. But not for long. About ten miles out of San Jose Helen switched on the light and began to write. Holding the notepad for me to read, she tilted her chin defiantly and stared into the night.

The note said, "I swallowed a whole bottle of phenobarbs."

I was incredulous. I wanted to scream, "What the hell are you up to?" Instead, I asked quietly, "When? What time?"

"Just before you arrived. Before we went to the Derby." The set of her jaw and her concentrated gaze into the night seemed to say, "It wasn't very nice of me, but there's nothing you can do about it."

"How many did you take? What size were they?"

Helen shrugged as if she didn't intend to be pinned down to details.

"Damn it, Helen. Why did you do this?"

Slowly she turned to me, her eyes innocent and questioning.

"How many did you take?"

She measured about two inches in the air between thumb and forefinger.

I pulled to a stop on the freeway shoulder. "Helen, that doesn't mean a damned thing to me. How many pills? Twenty? Thirty?"

She wrote, "50 1/2-gr tablets." Her attitude added doubt to the estimate.

"Are you sure you took that many?" I wondered if she had taken any at all. I was weary. But here I was; there was no escape.

Helen nodded yes unconvincingly and wrote, "They don't affect me much. I have a tolerance for them."

"Why do you tell me about it if you have a tolerance for fifty?" I was furious. First the bar, and now this. "Helen, you've taken enough to kill yourself. We're going back to the hospital."

She reached for the car door and shook her head vigorously.

"If you took that many pills you're going to need good medical care."

She scrawled, "I'll jump out if you turn back."

I closed my eyes and leaned back. How much crazier could this night become? Guided by my intuition, I pulled onto the freeway in the direction of my home.

My state of mind didn't improve with the miles. Emotions of a lifetime surfaced. I knew that Helen was depressed. The doctor had told her frankly, as she had asked to be told, that she was not likely to live more than a few years. She had no speech. Tom, her lover and steady companion, had had a heart attack when her need for him was greatest. Yet this overdose didn't seem genuine. But I couldn't be sure. Helen had repeatedly gambled with life, revved it up with risks, even as she now drew cigarette smoke and alcohol over the fragile tissues in her throat. Was she gambling that fifty pills were not too many? Would she jump out if I turned back?

I didn't live as a physician twenty-four hours a day. I was different things to different people; now to Helen a sister. But surely I should regard her as a patient with an overdose and turn back to the hospital.

A year and a half ago I might have cooperated with Helen in a suicide plan. I wondered if that's what I was doing now. I remembered well the day her doctor phoned me to describe the proposed surgery, to alert me to the possibility of complications and to be sure I understood the poor prognosis. At that time the growth on her vocal cord had already been treated with radiation and had outlived its effects to sprout like a mushroom in the back of her throat. Sick at heart, I had considered her alternatives: no further treatment and a ghastly death from suffocation and starvation, or mutilating surgery with loss of speech, and death postponed only a short time. It occurred to me that she might opt for a third choice—suicide. That this solution apparently did not occur to her surprised me.

Now as we neared home I found myself recalling Don Marquis' creation Mehitabel, the proud alley cat whose soul had previously incarnated in Cleopatra. Mehitabel who sang,

> i know that i am bound
> for a journey down the sound
> in the midst of a refuse mound
> but wotthehell wotthehell
> oh i should worry and fret
> death and i will coquette
> there's a dance in the old dame yet
> toujour gai toujour gai

Helen did not become drowsy. A few blocks from my home she wrote, "I'm hungry. Let's find a restaurant."

"We can fix something at home."

Helen shook her head, frowned, and mouthed that "dinner" was what she had in mind, adding with a woebegone expression, "I haven't eaten all day."

This was too much. "Helen, you're telling me that you haven't eaten all day and that you took a bottle of phenobarb's hours ago. And you're not getting drowsy. This adds up to just one thing: you're playing me for a fool."

She wasn't accustomed to anger from me. She jerked herself away, and shook her head in denial.

I spotted a Denny's still open at midnight. Helen ordered a ham dinner. I ordered tea and toast. She poked disdainfully through the salad she couldn't swallow as she waited for the entree. I sipped tea and nibbled at the toast. I was tired and in no mood to attempt conversation. She looked about at the empty booths, the deserted counter, the lone waitress and seemed to find them wanting. Then she settled into her meal. She cut the ham into small pieces and dipped each piece into the mashed potatoes and gravy to make them easier to swallow. Looking more and more dejected she finally pushed the plate from her, most of the food uneaten. She looked about as if Denny's had let her down. The waitress was solicitous. Helen's expression said, "It's too late now for your concern."

At home she suggested phoning our sister Betty who lived only five miles away. She had been Helen's reliable lifelong ally within the family. Now widowed and with six children, she was less accessible to Helen than I was. Besides, when Helen had last visited Betty a couple of weeks ago the bedlam in Betty's house had driven her to the nearest bar, and then to an early bus home. Now they both harbored ill feelings which they both shared with me.

"It's 1 A.M., Helen. We can wait until daylight to call Betty." I dropped into an easy chair, then thought better of prolonging my wakefulness and said, "Let's head for bed." I got up and started to the guest room that had twin beds. "I'm a light sleeper. I'll wake up if you need me during the night." She considered the bed and indicated she wasn't sleepy. She sat down, turned on the radio and picked up a magazine.

I lay down on one of the beds and quickly fell asleep.

I was awakened by Helen's nudging and the notepad held before me. "Let's go shopping tomorrow. You have a Nordstrom's here, don't you?"

"Let's get some sleep first . . . Isn't that an expensive store?"

Helen pulled a roll of tens and twenties from her purse, held them before me and wrote, "I want to buy you a nice dress. You never buy pretty things for yourself."

I squeezed her hand in appreciation, and wondered where the money came from. She lived on a small disability check from the government.

A few minutes later the notepad again, "Do you have any brandy in the house?"

Sleepily, "We'll get some when we go out tomorrow."

With the music on the radio I slept, but with each interruption of the announcer's voice I stirred and saw Helen sitting there writing.

"Do you think I could shorten my white knit coat while I'm here?"

Which meant, "Would you shorten it for me, Kay?" Helen didn't sew.

Yet another note. "I'm my doctor's favorite patient. He's the best ENT surgeon in N. Calif. I couldn't have had better medical care. Would you believe - my bill at the hospital this past year, for 1970, was over $20,000?"

Drowsily I thought, *MediCal is intended for people like you. You've worked all your life. If you hadn't used so many aliases you'd have a social security income.* But I said nothing to detract from Helen's fancied accomplishment of getting MediCal to spend $20,000 on her.

As the dark of the sky gave way to gray, Helen motioned, "I'm going outside to have a cigarette."

And so morning came.

- Chapter 3 -

We'd shop early. "But not for a dress for me," I said. "I'm simply not in the mood. Another time maybe."

Helen acknowledged my pronouncement with an "if you say so" expression and no apparent disappointment.

I was too miserably tired to puzzle for long over the night before, so unreal, yet so like Helen. I'd never understood what motivated her. But I knew she needed me and that I would not make my help contingent on her reforming. That was not only unlikely but impossible.

At ten o'clock our feet were sinking into the thick carpeting of Nordstrom's Better Fashions room. Helen seemed to belong in a place like this. I didn't.

"I love your taste in clothes, your flair for dressing," I told her as I marveled at the harmony of color in the apricot knit pant-suit, the burnt- orange scarf, the peach tint of her facial make-up, and her auburn hair.

"I won this suit on a bet at the Derby," she wrote.

I noticed too how her distinctive gait marred her attractiveness. I'd never liked the way she thrust her knees back assertively with each step, making her movement awkward.

I expected to help Helen communicate with the clerks in the

store. But tipping her chin high she beckoned a saleslady. Supplementing written messages with mouthed words and gestures, she quickly had the attention of several sales clerks eager to help her. I watched fascinated as she was demanding one moment, charming the next.

In the dressing room with several suits to try on, she explained to me, "Size 14 fits my hips but 12 is better for the jacket."

"It's no problem. Buy the correct jacket size. The slacks are easy to alter." Then, forgetting my intention to rest later, I added, "We can do it this afternoon."

Helen tried on first one suit, then another, critically appraising each before the mirror. She frowned, tugged here and there, for a moment pleased, then took off each outfit with an air of dissatisfaction.

Becoming weary as the morning wore on, I wondered why a choice was so difficult. With her thin legs, her large waist, and the roll of skin for grafting dangling immodestly against her breast, what difference did it make, size twelve or size fourteen? Coral or rust? Never mind. Surely I could accept her foibles at such a difficult time.

She finally selected a suit for the season of silky cotton broadcloth of an unusual peach-pink blend. It was long-sleeved with a loose-fitting jacket and straight pants. She sat down on a stool in the dressing room and took a tiny pair of scissors from her purse. Was she going to switch price tags from a less expensive suit to this one? As she brought her little scissors near the garment, I grabbed her arm. "Helen. what are you doing?"

She jerked her arm away from me and angrily pointed out that it was only a size label she intended to change.

"Oh, for Christ's sake," I said, "if you want to pull this kind of thing I'll leave you to shop by yourself. You can take a cab home."

Was Helen's foremost desire to have a well-fitting suit or did she want this small triumph over Nordstrom's? In the last year I'd observed the importance to her of small "wins." Recently, until the laryngectomy made her speechless, she had seemed to delight in cheating Bell Telephone out of its charges. She'd phone me person to person, often around midnight, often when she'd been drinking. I'd rouse myself and ask her, "Is something wrong? Why are you calling at this hour?"

"Oh, I was just telling Sam here about you. Kay, say 'Hello' to Sam."

Hearing the jukebox music and the jarring sound of voices, I'd answer irritably, "Why would I want to say 'Hello' to Sam, whoever he is? If you want to talk for a few minutes . . ."

"Kay, honey, don't be that way. Here, Sam say 'Hello' to my little sister."

Being civil with effort, I'd say something like, "It's nice to talk to you, Sam. Take good care of Helen."

I tried to end one such call tactfully with, "This must be costing you a lot," only to learn the truth weeks later from a long distance operator.

"Did you receive a call from someone in San Jose?"

"Uh . . . I can't remember," I hedged

"Do you know anyone in San Jose?"

"Uh . . . I know a lot of people."

"Would you know a Victor Young?"

Victor Young was Helen's last husband. I said, "No." Angry as I was with her I couldn't bring myself to tell the phone company that Helen, hoarse from cancerous vocal cords, was undoubtedly Victor Young. But, damn, why did she put me in a spot like this?

Now in the dressing room, Helen's eyes and her quivering lower lip showed that she felt hurt, piqued by my righteous attitude, unfairly accused. Then she gathered up the clothes, their markers intact, and presented the one she'd selected to a clerk. When that lady completed wrapping the suit she handed it to Helen in silence, sympathy and admiration on her face.

As we walked away from the sales counter, Helen winked at me. "They do it all the time," she wrote, elaborating on the comment with a quick movement of her finger to her mouth, then a cupped hand behind her ear, another wink and a shake of her head, all of which said, People mean well, but they're stupid to think I'm deaf just because I can't talk.

In the parking lot she scribbled, "The brandy."

That noon at home she wrote, "You're tired. I'll get lunch. As soon as I've had a cigarette. And would you call the Derby and find out how Tom is?"

The word from the hospital to the Derby and then to me on the phone was that Tom had improved but was not yet ready to go home.

"I should get back in the morning to see him. I'll find out from a connection I've got at the hospital when his wife visits. No need running into her."

"You've known Tom a long time."

"Ever since Vic walked out on me fifteen years ago. He's the best man I ever had. Better than any of my husbands." After a moment's pause she resumed writing. "He's considerate in so many ways. Did I ever tell you he arranged for us to have a joint bank account?" She seemed tired and placed the pad on the table. A few minutes later, with a thoughtful expression, she picked up pencil and pad to say, "Strange how sickness changes things. Sex isn't important any more."

We both slept for a few hours after lunch. I'd not lost sight of my having to be at the hospital early Monday morning. Helen had decided not to see Betty on this visit. After our naps she tried on the handsome new peach-pink suit. I was relieved that it fit to her satisfaction. I wouldn't have to pull out threads and open up the sewing machine.

The next morning, Sunday, Helen was up with the sun, packing the few things she had brought with her into her suitcase for the trip home. I was relieved that she wanted to take the Greyhound bus.

The downtown streets near the bus depot were deserted. The depot's waiting room was empty except for an old man dozing on a bench, and Saturday night's litter not yet swept up. Helen, impeccably dressed, viewed the scene with a shake of her head. I went directly to the ticket window. But Helen elbowed me aside decisively and with a smile that acknowledged my good intentions. Importantly she wrote, "San Jose," and pushed the note under the window to the ticket agent.

As we sat on a wooden bench to wait for the bus she wrote, "Don't worry about me. I'll be all right." I said, "I'll trust you to have someone call me if you need me, or just to let me know how you are."

Then she was on the bus, sitting in a window seat, bright and smiling. I waved; she blew a kiss. I stood there watching her until the bus pulled out.

<h1 style="text-align:center">- Chapter 4 -</h1>

LATE APRIL AND EARLY MAY WERE BUSY WEEKS FOR ME. BESIDES going to the hospital daily I was planting a garden which should have been started a month earlier. And there was my eleven-year-old son who was almost solely my responsibility. Like other suburban mothers I spent a lot of my leisure time toting him around to endless extra-curricular activities. Fortunately I'd chosen a profession where I could work less than full time and still have enough income for our modest life style. I'd been happy for a few years with his father, my second husband, before we were married. When our relationship became legal it shriveled like a leaking balloon and ended in divorce. One Saturday morning, satisfied that home and work could be neglected for the day, I drove to San Jose to spend a few hours with Helen. I hadn't seen her for several weeks, since the phony overdose episode and the upsetting morning at Nordstrom's. I stopped first at the Derby and, not finding her there, walked the half block to her house. The front door into her kitchen was open. I rattled the screen door, then pressed my face against it to see inside. Helen waved to me from where she sat on a pillow on the kitchen floor. The "old trunk" was beside her in the middle of the room, moved from its usual place against the wall, its top open and supported on a chair, its contents scattered on the floor about it.

"Ugh, the past." I grimaced at the sight of the relics. A musty odor filled the room. Then I laughed and said, "No, it's not that bad. But first, tell me, how are you, and how's Tom?"

Helen frowned, gave a shrug and wrote, "I guess Tom's all right. He's home, says he's too tired to spend much time here. And I don't have the energy to go to his place like I used to. I phone him almost every day from the Derby."

"And you?"

She shrugged and indicated that for the moment she was occupied.

"You're hardly alone with all these keepsakes." My eyes wandered over the mementos that surrounded her: the sepia photographs, the worn envelopes full of snapshots that had been sorted and put there by our mother years ago, a variety of frayed and yellowed papers, a rosebud vase of milk glass, a set of baby's tarnished silverware.

The "old trunk," as our family called it, had been carried from Pennsylvania to Ohio and on to Wisconsin by our long-deceased grandparents. When Mother and Dad died in 1944, my first year in medical school, I was still struggling to free myself of restrictive family ties. Consequently, I claimed no family possessions. Helen and Betty took what they wanted; what happened to the rest no one seems to know. Soon after that the antiquated chest came to California with Helen, the first in the family to go West. The sight of it now in Helen's room distressed me, reeking as it did of a past I still wanted to forget. Although this project invited my participation, I was reluctant. For Helen it seemed a fascinating activity. She prided herself on her memory of long ago events, even the trivial happenings—Aunt Mattie breaking a tooth on a plum seed, Betty crashing her bike into the woodpile—forty years ago.

I expected her to bring up the death of little Boots, our toy bull dog, with the accusation, "You didn't even shed a tear." It was true. As Mother and my sisters sobbed and wailed, I stood there, an unfeeling observer. I'd never played with Boots, never cuddled her; that was for the others. Dad, solemn and silent, had dutifully buried her. I had learned early to regard Dad and me as strong and rational, Mother and my sisters as weak and emotional.

Now as Helen and I contemplated the contents of the trunk, it occurred to me that my reluctance to confront the past was as bad as her preoccupation with it. With resolve, I said, "I'll join you."

Sunlight poured into the kitchen through front and side windows, tempering the dankness of the old trunk.

"The sun makes this room very cheery."

Helen looked about as if only this minute perceiving the golden light that flooded the room.

"Time drags when I don't have the energy to go out," she wrote.

"Time won't be a problem for awhile, Helen. You could spend weeks going through this stuff." I settled onto a pillow beside her.

My eyes lit on a photograph of our father. "Why, we could spend a day just talking about Dad." I paused. "But thinking about him makes me sad."

Dad's life had been a series of lost opportunities. It was always too late. Too late for a career in law, too late to make the move West that we dreamed of every spring and, marrying at age forty-seven, almost too late for a family. With dejected finality, he'd pronounce, "Well, for me it's too late now." These words became a theme that ran through our lives, and influenced me with the inference that it needn't be too late for us children.

I looked long and thoughtfully at the photograph of the handsome man with the defiant eyes, the jauntily tipped hat, the cigar in his mouth.

"That was his campaign picture," Helen mouthed as she pointed to the face that challenged us.

"Imagine a crook like Dad running for sheriff. But that's not fair. I suppose he wasn't really a crook. But he did have a compulsion to outwit everyone. Giving a horse with heaves a shot of adrenaline to keep it breathing long enough to sell it. Shooting craps with loaded dice."

"He knew what was right for everyone else," Helen wrote.

"Yes, and for himself, too. But right for him was his own distorted view of it."

"He loved the troubles that repeatedly took him into court where he could act as his own lawyer."

All through our childhood we'd loved story-time with Dad. It was a time without reprimands or arguments, a time when we took turns sitting on his lap, glad he was our father. As we grew older the stories took on a real life character.

"Remember the tale about how he and his girlfriend, the school teacher, stole grapes along the road one moonlit night? How old Murphy blabbered that they'd stolen the grapes, and how Dad bearded the old man in the saloon and forced him to retract his story? I think I remember that yarn because it troubled me."

Helen looked puzzled.

"I mean it's a pretty morally confusing tale."

She seemed to ponder my words before penning a reply. "I marveled at the sheer guts and bluff with which he pushed people around."

"And controlled us."

"Oh, I don't know about that," Helen mouthed. "I managed to do a lot of things he never found out about."

I considered that and, thinking of our childhood, asked, "Like roller-skating?"

Among the many presents Aunt Mae sent us, the roller-skates were our favorites. Dad, ever fearful that we'd hurt ourselves, forbade us to use them. I remembered one day when Dad's footsteps outside the door brought our conversation about the skates to an abrupt end. Mother pushed her chair from the table and motioned to Betty to cover her bruised knees. I reached into the sewing box for a sock to mend. Helen grumbled, "There's never anything to do around here."

Dad caught her words as he came in the door. "Do what a young lady should do," he warned. "Sit in a chair and behave.

Mother and I do the best we can to bring you up right. Now don't let me hear another word out of you."

He stood there, a slender, slightly stooped man, ready to take on his family. His customary three day growth of beard, his brown corduroy pants held up by suspenders, and a worn brown wool sweater gave him the appearance of a man who sacrificed for his family.

Mother said, as she had so many times, "But, Dad, they've got to do something."

"They don't," he retorted, "not the things they want to do, not roller-skating, not swimming. They're girls."

His voice rose. His eyes bore down on us; he thrust a finger at Mother. "What have you done with those roller-skates? They could break their necks on those abominations. I told you to ship them back to their Aunt Mae."

Betty pulled her dress more tightly against her knees. At such times we'd all wonder if Dad was about to have a tantrum. They were fearsome spectacles to which the damaged furniture attested: an absent stained glass panel in our only table lamp, a jagged tear in the front of the leather upholstered chair. But, as a "matter of principle" Dad never struck a woman. So, except for spankings, the hallmark of a good parent, we knew he would never lay a hand on us.

"You heard me," his voice threatened. "They're not to wade either. That river's treacherous. It was only half a mile from the picnic area that Ed Connelly's boy drowned."

Reference to that tragedy of a few years earlier added to our uneasiness. Dad had been up half the night dragging the river for the body of his friend's nine-year-old boy. Mother and we three children were there on the grass huddled under the trees with dozens of other women and their little ones. The river flowing through the town at this point became a straight steep-banked channel known as "the race." Grim men along the bank were silhouetted against the black river by the eerily darting beams of flashlights. It was almost dark when the search began. Except for a shout now and then from the men to each other there was silence—a quiet filled more with dread than with hope.

Then Dad came up to us and said, "Take them home, Mother."

Several hours later we were still waiting up when Dad walked in. He didn't look at any of us. He pulled off his gloves and headed for the stove where he stood rubbing his hands together. "How about some hot coffee, Mother?" His voice was flat; he was shivering. We couldn't tell if it was from the cold or maybe from seeing the body. What did a drowned boy look like, I wondered. Mother poured coffee and sat down at the table. She was silent. We could tell she wanted to make Dad feel better. We waited, wondering, not daring to ask. "Go to bed, girls," Dad said. We had never heard his voice sound so tired.

Now, finished with admonishing Mother, he turned to us. "So, have I made it clear? You're not to put a foot in that river." As he said it his look pierced the eyes of each of us in turn.

Then he relaxed, picked up the newspaper and sat down in the rocking chair. "Well, it looks like Al Smith will be the next president," he commented in a new voice. "That is, if there aren't too many people like your mother out there voting for Hoover." He winked and looked over his glasses at us girls.

"We managed to do a lot of roller-skating but we never learned to swim," Helen wrote.

"No, but things got better. Dad mellowed."

Helen nodded agreement.

"Interesting, isn't it, that we all wanted to grow up to marry a man like Dad."

"And I succeeded three times," Helen mouthed, holding out three fingers. "Thank God Tom finally came along."

- Chapter 5 -

"Let's stretch. My legs are stiff from sitting so long." I got up awkwardly and reached a hand to Helen. "Do you have any tea?"

She motioned that I should look around and help myself to anything I wanted.

The cupboards were so nearly bare that the choice was not difficult. This didn't surprise me; even when she was well, her cupboards had little but an odd assortment of dishes and such staples as crackers and pretzels.

In the refrigerator I found a dozen eggs and a carton of half and half. In response to my unasked question, Helen wrote, "The nurse insisted I buy them to put a little fat on me." She pulled up a pants leg. I looked away recalling the many compliments paid those once shapely legs.

"I can't eat." She indicated nausea.

"I'll make you an eggnog you can't resist."

"Don't waste your time," she mouthed.

But she seemed to know, as in the years of our childhood, that I would insist on what I thought was good for her. She shrugged, then smiled as if to accept the inevitable.

I served us tea, and to Helen a small glass of eggnog. She

seemed at first to enjoy the tea. But its lack of calories concerned me. She tasted the eggnog.

"Not bad, eh?" I prompted.

She shrugged and pushed it from her.

"Helen, you've got to eat to live. You can make yourself eat. You're not half trying. Hell, I could eat shit if that's what it took to keep me alive."

Such words had been forbidden in our family, and I couldn't bring myself to utter a one of them until the '60s when they were already appearing on bumper stickers.

She looked up quickly and held her eyes on me for a few seconds. Then she tipped the glass to her lips, contorted her face to swallow, and was again expressionless.

Her slow pace at times like this taxed me. I felt a need to fill silences with words, still times with motion. Aware of my impatience, I determined to sit quietly, to be with Helen completely, with the painful passageways of mouth and throat, with the body I hoped would transform this food into flesh. I was lost in reverie when Helen held her notepad before me.

"Sometimes I feel that what's left of life isn't worth it."

"If you really don't want to eat, it's OK."

We sat there a few minutes longer. I put the food away, then went over to the trunk. Let's look at some pictures here at the table. I'll bring them over."

I handed her a picture of Mother with us three little girls. A radiant buxom woman in her late thirties, energetic and proud, stood in the sun among the autumn leaves. An elegant suit with a fitted jacket and a long skirt enhanced her natural dignity. We played beside her in our velvet coats, hats, and matching muffs.

"We still had money when that was taken," Helen observed.

"Indeed, but not for long after that."

Mother was one of five daughters born to a strong-willed seamstress and a gentle hack driver. From the age of sixteen she'd been a country school teacher and, in the summer months, a student at the Chicago Conservatory of Music. At thirty, ignoring the wishes of her sisters, she married Dad, a gambler, horse trader, and real estate dealer seventeen years her senior. They settled down on a small farm in the Swiss cheese country of southern Wisconsin.

Three years later, in 1916. their first child, a boy, was still-born. I arrived a year after that. It wasn't long before Dad described me as a chip off the old block and was confident I'd be a satisfactory substitute for the boy he'd wanted.

Two years later Helen came along. An adorable bubbly baby, they said. Already in the early years there were hints of the traits that would perplex those about her all her life. A spirited child, she made up to people quickly, laughed and cried with equal ease, was tender-hearted and quick-tempered. She sputtered and screamed, kissed and hugged, and never held a grudge.

When I saw what Helen had done I ran into the house to get Mother. "Come quick. Helen is squashing the rabbits."

Already at age five I'd learned to react with control.

"Oh, dear." Mother rushed to the front porch where two baby rabbits lay lifeless. Helen was sitting on a third one. Mother grabbed her, too late to save the little animal. "That's very naughty," she said, swatting her bottom. "What will Dad say?"

Helen threw herself on the floor, cried lustily, and kicked her feet against the floor boards. Mother put the three dead pets into a galvanized pail. "When he gets home Dad will dig a hole to bury them."

Helen jumped up, gleeful. "I help. I get my shovel and dig." Then, reaching up toward Mother, "I love you, Mommy," she giggled, snuggling against Mother's leg.

During Mother's next pregnancy she discovered a small growth on her upper lip. The doctor diagnosed a benign cystic tumor and removed it with electric cautery. The treatment didn't entirely take care of the matter. Dad, who on principle distrusted his fellow man, singled out doctors for his deepest distrust.

Mother continued to worry. Tumor was an ominous word. Her own mother had died at the age of fifty-two from cancer of the uterus. She told us when we were older how she watched helplessly as her mother slowly weakened and bled to death. Graphically describing the blood-soaked pads and her mother's courage, she would collapse in shaking sobs as we huddled around her in silence.

The baby Betty was born two years after Helen and was as unlike us as we were unlike each other. A birthmark, a large bulbous upper lip that dripped blood whenever she fell, dominated her physical being and of course created enormous psychological hardship. Mother was convinced that the little tumor on her own upper lip had somehow caused Betty's disfigurement. Our parents were much too enlightened to hide their birthmarked child as was common among country folk at that time. They bore their guilt stoically. By the time Betty was four and children called her "pig snout" she, in effect, hid herself. From time to time Dad considered plastic surgery, once even arranging for a surgeon to examine the lip. But he always concluded that a surgeon couldn't be trusted not to make matters worse.

Little Charlotte, even though the trunk yielded up no evidence of her, was imprinted on our minds. She was stillborn, and we knew her for only those few moments when Dad and a neighbor carried her coffin to a car to be taken to the cemetery. We didn't know Mother was pregnant; her stout build and corseted trunk gave no hint of the child within. It was with surprise and awe that we three children looked into the white satin-lined coffin at the pale little face framed by lace ruffles and the tiny body in a long white dress that Mother had embroidered. More memorable even than this was the sight of Dad wiping a tear from his cheek.

As we sorted through the pictures in the trunk we found few of Betty. Over the years she had destroyed them, sometimes tearing only herself out of the snapshot, leaving everyone else. The appearance of the lip improved over the years. Repeated bleeding from injuries produced scar tissue and shrinkage so that within the family we hardly noticed it.

In a snapshot from the mid twenties that had eluded Betty's

scissors we looked at three pudgy little girls, their short straight hair draped to one side over a full cheek and secured by a barrette. Strands of Helen's hair had broken loose to brush against her face.

"They fed us well," Helen observed. "Thank God, we outgrew that Pennsylvanian Dutch cooking."

"Roast pork or roast beef and gravy. Not a vegetable that wasn't drowned in cream sauce. And remember the banana cream pies? No wonder Dad boasted that he fed his family well." I looked again at the picture. "I can see from your impish smile why Dad called you mischievous. This must have been about the time you disrupted Sunday dinner by lining up peas on your knife."

Helen shrugged, raised her eyebrows, and clearly didn't understand my reference.

When Helen was four and we lived on our little farm, the Knutsons, neighbors from down the road, came for Sunday dinner. While Mother prepared the dinner the adults visited in the living room and Helen engaged Mr. Knutson in bouncing her horsy-style on his knee. Each time he tired or slowed, she'd scream, "More, more," until Dad said sharply, "Enough." Instantly she slid to the floor.

At the table we filled our plates with fried chicken and gravy, mashed potatoes, and peas fresh from the garden in rich cream sauce. Everyone ate heartily; our guests murmured appreciation. Helen ate everything on her plate except her peas. Then she fidgeted until, as if suddenly inspired, she took her knife and carefully placed one pea after another on it. The knife with seven or eight peas aboard was poised before her open mouth when Dad's eyes caught her. Without a second's hesitation he pushed his chair back, grabbed her, and gave her bottom two stinging wallops. He carried her to the kitchen, plunked her down on a stool and returned to the table without a word. Her kicks and screams effectively disrupted the meal in spite of Dad's and Mother's pretense that all was well.

"Have some more chicken, Al," Dad urged.

"Yes, there's plenty more in the kitchen," Mother added.

Dad's eyes snapped at Mother as he warned, "Don't go near that kitchen."

As the noise became louder, he pronounced the expected threat. "One more sound out of you, and I'll give you something to cry about."

There was silence, not even a concluding sniffle from the kitchen.

Mother cleared the table onto the side board and brought on the apple pie. She placed a large piece of sharp Cheddar cheese on each plate beside the pie. Dad looked with pride and approval at the dessert. "I always say," he quipped, "pie without cheese is like a kiss without a squeeze."

We laughed.

Then he called to the kitchen, "Helen, if you know how to eat now, you may return to the table."

She sprang into the room, skipping. Looking at Dad she quickly converted to a walk. She flashed smiles around the table, shot seductive glances at Mr. Knutson, and resumed her place. Then her fork dug into her piece of pie.

As I related this Helen's eyes sparkled.

"In case you don't remember," I said, "Dad enforced impeccable table etiquette. I'm sure a knife in the mouth would have rated eight for bad manners on a scale of ten."

She shook her head and mouthed, "Strange, but I don't remember." Then she wrote, "It was probably just one of so many things I did that Dad didn't approve of."

She smiled and moved to pick up another picture.

- **Chapter 6** -

THE OLD TWO-STORY FRAME HOUSE WHERE OUR PLAY HAD WORN
thin the grass in the yard was our next reminder of the past.

"We lived in such dismal places after we sold the little farm,"
I commented.

"Dismal?"

"I certainly don't look back with nostalgia to those stark
houses with the outdoor privies. Or to the wood or coal-burning
stoves that heated either our front or back and never both. Or to
the water pumps that froze in the winter and had to be thawed
and primed." I could have gone on and on and included ecru lace
curtains, faded rugs, and naked light bulbs that hung by cords
from the ceiling.

"So? Those were the times," Helen wrote defensively.

"True," I admitted, "but a little coziness—a shade around the
light, a soft pillow in the rocking chair—would have helped."

Helen shrugged, "Maybe."

I wondered: was she indifferent, or had she been insensitive
to our early surroundings, or . . . ? A third possibility occurred to
me.

"Don't you like for me to criticize?"

She mouthed that she didn't care what I said, with a pout that convinced me of her objections.

"Do I sound as if I think I was too good for the rest of the family?" I tended to forget that Mother and my sisters used to accuse me of feeling that way.

She grabbed a pencil and wrote with gusto, "EXACTLY." and thrust the word before me.

I laughed. "I guess the truth is that I accepted our way of life along with the rest of you at the time. It was only later when far removed that I began to think how ugly and difficult it had been." Then, hoping to find accord with her, I added, "But I know we all hated the frequent moves from one town to another."

She nodded an unequivocal Yes.

When Dad could no longer make a living from real estate and horses he tried his hand, with essential help from Mother, at running restaurants and hotels in half a dozen little towns in southern Wisconsin and northern Illinois. Usually we didn't do well. Then Dad would convince himself of the prosperity awaiting us in a village thirty or forty miles away.

It would begin at dinner time. He'd clear his throat after a long silence and announce, "There's no way to make a living in this town." "Oh, Dad . . . ," Mother would begin to protest. We children would look into our plates and wonder with dread what new school we'd be attending. Dad would continue, "I just heard about a place where they need someone to run a hotel."

We knew it wouldn't be long before we'd be loading our belongings onto a truck, and cleaning an empty house for the next renter. We never challenged those unilateral decisions even when the failure of previous ventures proved his judgment terrible. At least one piece of furniture would have to be sold to pay the moving expenses. Mother would cry. I would have nightmares. Then we'd all settle into the new life.

"The most traumatic move for me was from Brodhead to Lone Rock. You were seven."

Brodhead and Lone Rock were the two places we kept returning to from the various other little towns where Dad was lured by fantasies of making a decent living. Brodhead was a neat predictable farming community of about 1200 straight-laced, well-off citizens. I say citizens in confidence because it is inconceivable that an outsider could have existed in that homogeneous population whose forebears had left the British Isles long ago and Switzerland more recently. Our roots were in Brodhead. That is where we went to Sunday School, marched in the Memorial Day parade, sold poppies for the veterans on Armistice Day, cheered for the basketball team, and walked up and down the main street on Saturday nights for want of anything better to do. No crime, no scandal spiced up life in that quiet village. It was much more Mother's kind of a town than Dad's.

Lone Rock was altogether different. Its very name hinted of beauty and desolation. Unlike that orderly rectangular town of Brodhead, it sprawled haphazardly out from a central cluster of stores and a bank and a hotel to the prairie on the north and to the river on the south. Its truly inspiring endowment was the Wisconsin River, a magnificent stream not remotely comparable to the race, Brodhead's swift straight channel that was the only other stream we'd ever seen. For miles the Wisconsin River flowed in a wide expanse between low sandy banks. Here and there it narrowed gorge-like and coursed spectacularly between cliffs of stratified pitted sandstone. Hidden from the eye were its treacherous sand bars which had lured many an unsuspecting swimmer to his death. Its backwaters flowed into the town, becoming a slough that overflowed its banks with the spring thaw, wasting to a swamp teeming with tadpoles by early summer. Less than a century before, the Sauk Indians had lived here in mystic harmony with the water, rocks, and wildlife.

In 1926, the year of our arrival, 423 people by census count were trying to eke out a living from the meager resources of this country. That year the hotel business boomed. The rooms were filled to capacity every night by construction workers building a new bridge across the Wisconsin River. This time Dad had led us to temporary prosperity.

Many of the town folk were like ourselves. But there were also exotic and frightening elements that fascinated us children:

the "river trash" in their barely habitable shacks, the handsome Winnebago Indian boy in my grade, and the tough kids at school who, more than any thing else, challenged our ability to adapt.

Looking again at the snapshot of us girls, aged five, seven, and nine, I said, "This was an exciting time in our lives."

Helen nodded enthusiastic agreement.

"Remember how we learned to fight and how proud of us Dad was?"

Until then we'd engaged only in bickering disagreements with our classmates. They'd taunt, "Dumbbell."

"Smart aleck" or "fraidy cat," we'd yell back.

And soon we'd all tire of the exchange.

In Lone Rock the kids were different: they fought for blood. When big Edith from down by the river pushed me off the sidewalk and threatened to make mashed potatoes of my face, I felt a new kind of fear. One afternoon, as we three sisters were about halfway home, Edith began to push and bully us. Without any prior plan I whispered to Helen, "I'll hold her while you hit her." I couldn't have held her for long, but I didn't need to because Helen responded immediately with a smashing blow to Edith's face. Then we ran as fast as we could toward home.

Safe in our living quarters at the hotel, we locked ourselves in the upstairs bathroom to speculate on the consequences of our attack, and to plan. Our whispering was interrupted by a loud rap on the door.

"Come out of there," Dad ordered. "I want to talk to you."

We opened the door and faced him, terrified. "Ed Saunders is downstairs, says you girls beat up his daughter, gave her a black eye and a bloody nose. He's threatening to beat me up if you don't apologize." He lowered his voice and drew us close. "Tell me the truth, girls. And remember, I don't want you being bullied by the likes of Ed Saunders' kids. Now, on the other hand, if . . . . ."

We suddenly knew Dad was on our side. When we told him exactly what happened, he winked and gave us each a pat on the shoulder.

When he went back downstairs to face Edith's father, we hid

and listened.

"Ed, I didn't bring up my girls to fight. But your daughter's been pushing them around ever since we've been here. They're not taking it any longer. And I want you to know I'm behind them. I'm a reasonable man, Ed, but if a fight's what you want, I'll give it to you." As Dad took off his glasses and began to push up his sleeves, Ed suddenly became conciliatory. He mumbled something about checking out our story with Edith as he backed out the door.

After that we became friends with Edith. We'd walk home together while she amused us with stories of her exploits and held us spell-bound with descriptions of the sex play she shared with her younger brother.

Once the bridge was built the construction crew left. The owner of the hotel, old Doc Hennessey, went back on his promise to renew our lease; so we too moved on. We lived in several other small towns before returning to Lone Rock to run a restaurant. Again, we stayed only a year. That year was filled with memories out of proportion to the short stay.

"Remember the afternoon we picked violets with Mother along the railroad tracks? Those tracks fascinated us. Where could they take us?"

Helen wrote, "That fall they took us all the way to the Wisconsin River."

"The forbidden exciting river. We rolled in the leaves, and then gathered nuts that we carried home in our petticoats."

Helen's face lit with recollection. "Only to find when we got home that they were inedible bitternuts."

"Which didn't detract at all from the adventure."

A soft smile spread over Helen's face and she seemed lost in reverie. Then her awareness returned to the room and, enlivened, she penned, "The winter of the big blizzards."

"Ah, yes. Horses and bobsleds replaced automobiles and Dad was in his heyday. "

The unprecedented heavy snow of that winter buffeted the little town, closing the school and all but one main road. The demand was urgent for horse drawn cutters and bobsleds. Dad opened a livery stable. Just when he would have given his bottom dollar for a few more horses, an Indian named Foran from North Dakota showed up in town with a string of harness horses. Dad had met the fellow several times in southern Wisconsin and northern Illinois. He was well known in the rodeo circuits. The two men made a deal and, in the month before the weather broke, they did a land office business.

It was then, when the cars again took to the roads, that Dad came home agitated, threw his gloves on the table, and said, "That son-of-a-bitch Foran double-crossed me." He paced around the kitchen rubbing his hands and we began to feel his worry.

"If Foran was a white man, I could handle him. But an Indian! They're sly as a weasel. No telling what trick he might pull on me."

He went through the house and pulled down all the window shades. Then he called Mother into their bedroom for a whispered conversation. When they came out Dad held a small pearl-handled pistol in his hand. We'd never before seen him look afraid.

"I've never met a man I couldn't whip with words. But now?"

Bedtime came, with our questions and fears unexpressed. Without the ritual bedtime kisses we went to our bedroom. During the night Betty mumbled and made eerie sounds that kept me from forgetting.

In the morning Dad announced, "We're going to the county seat so I can get a warrant for Foran's arrest. Hogan from down at the newspaper office will take us."

When we were ready to leave, Dad dropped the gun into his overcoat pocket and pulled a gray stocking cap over his head. The cap surprised me and added gravity to the situation. I'd never before seen Dad in a cap. He was a man who wore a hat during most of his waking hours, a brown felt hat with a brim that curved up in the back and dipped jauntily over one eye, taking on the world. The knit cap, reaching to his eyebrows, disguised and, I thought, disgraced that head. In the back seat of the sedan he slouched down between Helen and me as if to make himself invisible. Mother, with Betty on her lap, sat in front beside the driver. Our fear was almost palpable as we drove between the banks of snow along the county road toward the courthouse.

Dad got the warrant for the Indian's arrest without difficulty only to find on our return home that Foran and the horses had vanished across the prairie.

"But Dad redeemed himself the following summer," Helen wrote.

And I knew what she was referring to. Dad had never forgiven old Doc Hennessey for reneging on his agreement to lease us the hotel for another year.

Hennessey was not only a professional man, a dentist, but also a deacon in the Methodist Church. And, as we'd heard Dad say many times, he was a hypocrite and a liar.

Helen seemed to relish our recollection of that brawl on the town's main street.

It happened right below the big window of the living room of our flat above the restaurant. Mother heard a commotion below and looked out. "Oh, no!" she screamed as she rushed to the stairway. We got to the window in time to see people lead away the bloodied Doc. Then Dad came up the stairs.

Helen mouthed and mimed, "I can still see him, hands and face covered with blood."

The fight must have exhausted him (he was 65 years old) because he sat at the sink and let Mother wash away the blood and dab peroxide on his torn skin.

"It was the quiet of the scene that stayed with me," I said. "Dad explained nothing, Mother asked nothing. And we kids kept our distance, afraid to look until Mother called, "C'mon, girls, Dad's all right now."

With the blood gone he looked pretty good. We could make out a cut above Dad's right eye and a loose flap of skin hanging from his right jaw. But our relief was short-lived. Within the hour word reached us that Doc Hennessey was gravely injured. None of us spoke the dread that was surely on our minds.

In another week it seemed apparent that the Doc was recovering. After that, a lot of people thanked Dad for giving the old hypocrite what he had coming.

"Dad prided himself on getting his opponent to back down before a blow was struck. Wit and words were his weapons. I don't think he really wanted any other kind of a fight," I said. "I guess he'd been seething too long about old Doc Hennessey's going back on his word."

Helen nodded agreement..

It was well into the afternoon now. And Helen looked tired.

"I'm going to leave," I said, "and beat commute traffic. I hope Tom recovers so he can spend time with you soon." Glancing at the cup of tea and the eggnog still on the counter, I added, "I'd feel better if I thought you'd make an effort to eat."

She seemed to appreciate my concern and, pointing to the eggnog, wrote, "I promise."

- Chapter 7 -

The afternoon with Helen and the old trunk left me in an unsettled mood. Other memories surfaced. And the common theme was sex. It was a taboo subject in our family. On any other matter Dad spoke with conviction and at least a facade of authority. But in myriad ways he concealed and avoided anything that hinted of sex. By wearing long underwear the year around, even through Wisconsin's hot summers, he assured that his girls would see not so much as his bare legs, and certainly nothing to suggest that essential difference between the genders.

On the farm when a rooster took after a hen Dad would hurry us children away from the chicken yard with an urgency that intensified our interest. We satisfied our curiosity by watching the coupling of sparrows from the safety of our bedroom windows. While Helen and Betty whispered and giggled I was silently trying to bridge the gap between sparrows and people.

It was in the outhouse behind the little farm when I was six that I made a breakthrough discovery. We three children often gathered in the malodorous old two-holer to escape surveillance and share secrets, as well as to attend to the functions for which the privy was intended. On a day when little Keith and his family came to visit, he joined us in the privy. Helen was first to pull her dress up and her pants down and to jump onto the seat. We waited for Keith to go next. He turned to face the seat and, to my amazement, aimed a perfect arc of a yellow stream from himself into the hole in the toilet seat. I didn't see the source of this magic, and his matter-of-fact attitude only deepened the mystery. Helen shrieked, "Hey, how do you do that?" And little Betty probably was, as always, focused inward on her difficult baby world. I sensed that I had witnessed a truly significant event. To avoid embarrassment I told no one. Years passed before I appreciated what Keith had revealed that day.

When we reached high school Dad continued to protect us from dangers we could hardly imagine. He banned lipstick and forbade attendance at school dances.

"But times are different now, Dad," Mother protested.

He was adamant. "I don't care what's different. I know right from wrong for my girls."

Betty and I willingly stayed home with our books and our day dreams. Helen defied parental admonitions. Our parents, having no idea how to deal with Helen since rules and prohibitions didn't work, clung to the illusion that she was just a happy-go-lucky girl who would eventually straighten out.

When Helen was fifteen something happened that jolted them into the realization that she had gone far beyond the conventions of Brodhead. It might never have come to the attention of family or community if the boys had not left her alone late at night on a country road. The president of Brodhead's bank, driving home from a meeting, found her and brought her home.

Banker Mahoney, a rotund cheerful man and a pillar of righteousness in the town, didn't fear that Dad would point an accusing finger at him. He brought Helen home and told Dad, "I found your girl about ten miles out on the road to Beloit. I guess she had some trouble with her boyfriends. They left her to walk home." He chuckled self-consciously.

Dad was ill prepared for this development. His eyes scanned Helen uncertainly.

Mahoney turned to leave. "Not much more I can say. I hope

everything's all right."

Dad cleared his throat. "We're much obliged to you." He reached to shake Mahoney's hand.

Mother pulled Betty and me to the far side of the living room, leaving Helen and her father to confront each other where they stood near the front door.

"Don't look at me that way, Dad," Helen began irritably. "Hey, what's the big deal anyway? You're all staring at me."

Actually, more than looking at Helen, we were looking at each other, heavy with unease and suspense. Characteristically I felt guilty. Dad, his eyes burning into his daughter, had not spoken a word. Surely he would let go with a tongue lashing any minute.

Helen glanced at her clothes. Her skirt was a mess. The flowered blue print was wrinkled and dirty with road dust. A patch of stiffness looked as if the flaxseed gel we used to hold curls in our hair had spilled on her skirt. A faint odor of cigarette smoke drifted across the room, and a vague pungent odor I didn't recognize.

Helen said defensively, "The dirt will wash out. Gee, it isn't as if it's my best dress." An uneasy pause, "And I'm not hurt." She flexed her elbows and strutted a few steps before the immobile audience.

Finally Dad spoke, not with the rage I expected, but in a tired voice straining to be firm. "Helen, tell me what happened tonight. Who were you with? What's going on here?"

Shamelessly she looked into his face. "Well, when they pulled up in the car, I thought they were guys I knew." She fidgeted and glanced at the trio across the room. "When I got in I discovered I didn't know them."

"Were they Brodhead boys?"

She shrugged, "I dunno."

Dad bristled. "You don't know? What do you mean, you don't know?" Now he sounded more like himself.

"They were just boys. Hey, Daddy, don't ask me all these questions." Tears welled in her eyes. She looked again toward Mother and Betty and me.

"Don't look to your mother for sympathy." Then turning

toward his wife, "Mother, you stay out of this. I'll get to the bottom of it if it takes me all night. You and the girls go to bed." To Helen, "No one in this family's had a minute's sleep tonight for worry about you."

"Gee, Dad, you're making such a big thing of it. Leave me alone. I want to get some sleep too."

"You'll sleep when I get some answers."

Dad was an amateur sleuth for whom tackling mysteries from local scandals to head-lined murders was a pastime. He was especially drawn to intrigue that was likely to expose skullduggery by a respected person. But now, with his own daughter?

"Helen, it's not easy for me to talk about such things. But now that Mother and the girls have gone, did . . . ?" He glanced quickly at her before shifting his eyes away. "Did they do something to you?" Hearing his words seemed to embolden him. He repeated, "Did they do something to you?"

"Well," she shifted. "No . . . Not really."

"Not really? Helen, if they did, I'll have those sons-o-bitches behind bars. But you have to come clean with me."

Helen began to cry. "No, no, no, they didn't. I don't want to talk about it any more."

Maybe Dad had as little desire to hear more as Helen had to reveal anything. He slumped into a chair.

"Helen, your mother and I didn't raise you to be like this. You're bringing shame on the whole family." Then sternly, "You're to be home the minute school's out every day from now on. Do you hear what I'm saying? All right. Now clean up and go to bed."

Of course Mother and Betty and I had not gone to bed. We were as close to the living room as we dared be, straining to hear every word. If this incident had involved me two years ago at Helen's age I would not have got off so easily. Dad always held me accountable for everything. I was angry that Helen's punishment was so mild. But it was good that he had been reasonable and not a raving maniac. Yet I was uncomfortable, even sad, to witness his lack of confidence in dealing with my sister. I was as secure in my position as the good girl as Helen was in hers as the bad one. I just wanted Dad to be strong and sure of himself.

The next morning when Mother pressed Dad for information, he dismissed her with, "The less said the better."

She worried, "But if . . . well, I mean, maybe if . . . well, couldn't she be . . . ?"

Talk was inevitable. Mahoney was a sociable man. The dull little town didn't need much evidence to explode into gossip: "such a nice family," "the father's too strict," "they shouldn't hold that oldest girl up as an example all the time." As Mother and Dad and Betty and I pulled together protectively, Helen continued in her own orbit beyond the family nucleus, shrugging off the incident as if it hadn't happened.

We in the family discussed it neither among ourselves nor with others. Dad went about his affairs as usual except he had downcast eyes that avoided the questions in other eyes. Mother gathered us about her in the music room for more than our usual hours of piano and song.

Months passed without the consequence we secretly feared, and apparently without anyone's learning more than Helen and Mahoney had divulged that night.

- Chapter 8 -

In the fall of 1936 our family moved to Madison. With a student loan and a job with the National Youth Administration of Roosevelt's New Deal I had already completed one year at the University of Wisconsin. This next year would be easier. Our parents would run a student rooming house, and I would no longer live on the White Tower's six-cent hamburgers, Hershey chocolate bars, apples, and the occasional box of oatmeal cookies that Mother sent.

It was good to be home again. But I was troubled that Helen, almost seventeen-years-old, continued her by-now-established wayward life. In the evenings while Betty and I studied, she was out. We had no idea where she was.

One winter night when I was helping Mother with the dishes she lowered her voice and confided, "I've been beside myself with worry all day. I think Helen might be pregnant." Mother had confided in me since I was small. Isolated on a farm as we were in the early years there had been no one else, no friends or neighbors, to turn to. She had always watched over us children conscientiously, not as a meddler, but as a concerned mother. She knew when we each menstruated, just as in earlier years she knew when each had a bowel movement. Now she explained,

"Today when I emptied the waste basket in Helen's room I found a bag of sanitary napkins with each pad colored red with ketchup." She wiped the perspiration from her forehead and moved to face me. "I wouldn't bother you with this, dear, but I can't tell Dad. And Betty's too young."

This was too much for me. I was comfortable enough criticizing Helen for poor grades or late hours. But this! I had barely progressed from hand-holding to kissing. I dropped the dish towel and sat down on the kitchen stool. Shaken as I was I felt proud to be Mother's confidante.

"Maybe she has a boyfriend who'll help." It seemed unlikely but it was the only solution that came to my mind.

"I'll talk to her tomorrow," Mother resolved reluctantly.

The next evening we were all at the supper table when Helen bounced in. "Sorry I'm late," she said breathlessly as she pulled out a chair and sat down. With Helen's arrival Mother relaxed, ever occupied with smoothing over family differences. Dad's steel blue eyes did not leave his plate. It was so different from a few years ago when he'd have lectured Helen and then spanked her. Spankings had been a prominent feature of family life, the old-fashioned kind, administered on our bottoms and never in anger. Spankings of which our father said, "It hurts me more than it does you." Helen was the only one in the family or even outside of it who defied Dad. Somehow her defiance seemed unintentional, benign. Dad looked miserably ill-at-ease with this lack of control. Last week I heard him tell Mother, "Yet if I clamp down on her she may stray further. If only I could understand that girl."

No one said anything until Mother broke the tense silence. "How was school today?"

I felt no need to reply because I considered university to be beyond "school." Betty, who habitually said little, said nothing. Helen was probably thinking of the difficulty she would have getting out after supper, and said nothing.

Our father's stern voice jolted all of us to attention. "Your mother asked a question."

"I love French," I said. "We read aloud today."

Betty reported what our parents liked to hear. "I got the highest mark on the history test."

"We made muffins in cooking class," Helen said, adding a yum-yum gesture.

This conversation was going no where. We ended the meal in silence.

Tonight it was Helen's turn to help with the dishes. I gathered up my homework and pulled a chair to within listening distance of the kitchen.

Mother mustered her courage and got to the point quickly. "Helen, have you missed a period?"

"Why, no . . . Huh? . . . Well, what do you mean?"

"When I saw ketchup on your pads I assumed you wanted me to think you'd had a period when you hadn't." With distress mounting in her voice Mother pressed on, "Could you be pregnant?"

Without a break in her drying of the dishes, Helen said, "I don't know. I don't think so." She paused. "Maybe."

Mother took her hands out of the dish water, wiped them on her apron and, half-crying, said, "Helen, you can't be! What will Dad say?"

"Don't tell him."

"He has eyes. He'll see."

Helen took a plate from the dish rack. "There won't be anything to see."

With increasing anxiety Mother asked, "What do you mean?"

"If I'm pregnant, you don't think I'm going to stay that way, do you?" Helen lifted the pile of plates she had just dried and moved to put them into the cupboard. "Why don't we get a new set of dishes?" She examined several plates meticulously. "Look at the chips and cracks."

Mother persisted. "It's dangerous, isn't it, to . . . , to . . . ? Perhaps you could go out to California and stay with your aunt until it's over."

"Don't worry," Helen said irritably. "I'm not going anywhere.

I'll take care of it."

Helen's abdomen had been large in proportion to the rest of her body throughout childhood. And it had not shrunk to normal size in adolescence. "People may suspect, but it will be awhile before they can be sure. And that goes for Dad, too."

We agreed that Dad must not know. We didn't go so far as to speculate about what he might do should he find out. It seemed possible that Helen, with her years of misbehavior, might have worn him down to the point where he would forego histrionic threats and accusations. Thinking about Dad's reaction brought to mind a much earlier incident with another girl. I still felt bad about it because I was the one who told. The girl was eighteen, I was eight. Rita waited on tables and helped in the kitchen of a restaurant we ran in Orfordville. Dad always seemed uncomfortable around her, and critical. She curled her short hair to a frizz, wore skirts a full inch above her knees, and sang popular songs as she worked. Dad, though he had no ear for music, had become accustomed in our house to sounds of Beethoven and Mozart. Strains of "Yes! We Have No Bananas" and "It's a rain, rain, rainy day" grated on him. But he said nothing; in fact, he never spoke to or looked directly at the girl.

One evening after the restaurant was closed and Rita was the only one there, I went back to get some school papers I'd forgotten. When I walked into the kitchen I looked at Rita and completely forgot about my homework papers. She stood in the middle of the room in a pool of bloody water, her face flushed and perspiring. A galvanized pail was on the floor beside her, a mop in her hands. Red foot prints smudged the linoleum from the blood that trickled down her legs. Our eyes met for an instant before I ran from the room.

At home that night, after thinking about my discovery for a long time, I told Mother. The next morning Dad fired Rita.

When I was twelve I had a glimpse of a more tolerant father. In the various little towns where we lived we always became acquainted with the local doctor. We were often sick with colds.

And Dad, even as distrustful as he was of doctors, would still seek their advice. When we lived in a small town in northern Illinois Dad actually took a liking to old Doc Slattery. A decent, straightforward fellow who took care of people whether they had money to pay him or not, "a doc you could depend on for an honest answer," is the way Dad described him. So when Doc Slattery was sent to State Prison Dad was enraged. "A man of integrity rotting away in prison. It's this kind of injustice that makes me wish again that I'd gone to law school. A good lawyer could've got him off."

Of course, we children didn't understand the reason for Dad's diatribe. But when I was alone with Mother she explained that the doctor had helped a woman end her pregnancy. The woman already had five children and couldn't face the prospect of another one, Mother said. Unfortunately, the doctor's help was against the law.

Weeks passed. Helen didn't appear to be worried. In fact, nothing seemed to change, only that Mother's face became drawn. "What are you doing about it Helen?"

Helen brushed off the question.

Then one night in late February Helen came home and, finding only her mother and me up, dramatically placed her purse on the dining table and took from it a small rectangular box. "I got these from a guy I know," she said as she opened the box and displayed four huge black capsules. She lifted each out, fingered it, and then went to the kitchen for a glass of water.

"Are you sure you're supposed to take that many? Helen, they could harm you. You don't even know what's in them." Mother was worried.

"He says they worked for another girl. And you have to take that many if you want anything to happen. So," she added flippantly, "here goes."

I looked on, feeling inadequate that I had no advice for my sister as Helen swallowed the evil-looking capsules.

By midnight I heard her running to the bathroom. I lay in bed for hours listening to Helen moaning. Should I get up and try to help? What could I do? I really didn't want to be too close to whatever was happening. Besides, Mother was there. I stayed in bed, miserable.

The next day Helen slept all day.

"Is something wrong that Helen can't go to school?" Dad questioned.

"Seems like food poisoning," Mother lied. "She spent most of the night in the bathroom. She shouldn't go out in this cold."

By evening Helen was well—except that the life within her had weathered last night's storm.

"Damn," she complained to Mother.

"Helen, don't use that word. You'll let it slip out in front of Dad some day . . . What will you do now?"

Ten days later Helen produced another packet of pills. "Quinine. Better than those black devils. They work when nothing else does, or so I'm told."

The situation was telling on Mother. She was concerned not only with Helen's health, but was fearful that Dad might suspect her pregnancy.

The day after Helen took the quinine she was nauseated, dizzy, and had a constant humming in her ears. At the supper table that night she was pale and quiet.

"Eat, Helen," our father directed. "Your mother's prepared a meal any family could be proud of, and you're looking at an empty plate."

"I had a malted milk just before I came home. I forgot it was so late." She was the only one of us girls who could lie to our father.

He cleared his throat. We waited to see what punishment was in store for Helen for her ill-timed snack. But he said nothing. Everyone settled tensely into the meal and ate in silence.

That evening Dad stoked the furnace and went to bed early as usual. He was always up before the rest of us to have the house warm when we got up.

Helen allowed time for him to get to sleep. Then she began to run the bath water. This in itself was unusual; no one in our family took a bath in the middle of the week. Mother, already in her robe, tapped on the bathroom door. "What in the world is going on?"

After Mother went in, I opened the door a crack to satisfy my curiosity.

"It's supposed to work in hot water," Helen told Mother as she stepped into the tub. Quickly she jumped out and turned on the cold water until she could tolerate the temperature. As soon as she was comfortable in the half-filled tub she added hot water and more hot water until her submerged body became beefy red. "Mother, I forgot something. Please bring the mustard."

As Mother brought a large jar of mustard from the kitchen and handed it to Helen, she sighed, "Dear God, forgive me for being involved in this."

Helen emptied the mustard into the tub. Her perspiring face and shoulders rose from the water like a bronze bust from a saffron base.

"What will you do if this doesn't work?" Mother asked, as she pulled the faded chenille robe about her stout body and sat down on the toilet seat.

Helen began to cry. As the sobs continued, Mother leaned over her and tenderly kissed her wet cheek. "Don't cry, dear. I'm praying for things to work out."

For the women of this household to cope with anything on our own was a novel experience. Mother habitually consulted her husband who made every decision and arrived at every solution. Now we were without his advice. Mother's knowledge of pregnancy and childbirth was limited to her own difficult experiences. She had never known women who had abortions, and certainly had not been with women who talked of such things. I could contribute no help. Books were my dependable source of information, but as, a college sophomore, I was not about to venture into the medical school library looking for abortion material.

The next few weeks were uneventful. Then one day Helen announced, "There's a doctor in Janesville who does abortions. I have an appointment to see him tomorrow."

"But dear, where's the money coming from?"

"I'm just going for an examination. I'll tell him I want to know if I'm pregnant. Hah! suppose I'm not?" she giggled.

"Things can go wrong with abortions. It's already April. You're almost four months along." Mother wrung her hands and cast worried eyes into the distance.

The next evening, as Betty was setting the table and I was carrying the beef stew and coleslaw into the dining room, Helen walked in, much as she usually did, just in time for dinner. Impatient as Mother and I were for Helen's report, we dared not hurry the meal. Dad ate slowly and deliberately, to keep from choking, he said. No one deviated from the pace he set.

It was not until after the table was cleared and the dishes done that Helen had an opportunity to relate, "He examined me. He said he doesn't do abortions. He was a real nice guy. He said he thought I might have a miscarriage before long." She looked puzzled. "I couldn't figure out why he said that."

Mother sighed with discouragement.

Betty and I spread our papers and books on the dining room table and spent the next hour studying. Helen wandered about aimlessly.

By the time she began to have cramps Dad was asleep and Betty had gone to bed. Soon Helen was doubled up with pain, holding her belly with both hands. Mother and I were solicitous and frightened and, above all, hopeful. For the next hour Helen grimaced and rocked with recurring pain.

Finally she said, "I think I'll be better off in the bathroom," as she carefully moved to the toilet seat. Mother followed, trying to comfort her and dabbing at the perspiration that covered Helen's face. I stayed in the background. Suddenly, as she moaned louder than before, something dropped with a splash into the toilet bowl.

The cramps let up. Bright blood saturated the menstrual pads Mother had brought. Helen, pale and trembling, pulled a bath towel between her legs. With troubled eyes Mother helped her to the bedroom. Gradually the bleeding lessened and Helen, exhausted, settled into bed.

"Dear, that doctor must have done more than examine you," Mother suggested.

"He couldn't have," Helen said. "He only charged five dollars."

- **Chapter 9** -

Madison became home to our family. For me, living at home was certainly preferable to my first college year in a dormitory. But when a young student courted me and then proposed marriage I opted for what I thought would be an even better arrangement. We found an apartment within walking distance of my parents' rooming house. Mother liked my husband, but he wasn't exactly what my father had in mind for me (no man would have been). My sisters, with self-absorption typical of the teen years, hardly noticed my altered status. Betty, unobtrusive and studious, was within a year of her high school diploma. Helen graduated and, while continuing to live at home, began her career as a waitress.

She started at the Lake Hotel's Coffee Shop, moved on to the State Street Sandwich House, and a couple years later to Lenore's Cafe, located where the university campus merged with the downtown business district. It drew customers from both communities and afforded Helen an enviable opportunity to meet men. She dated but didn't settle into any steady relationship. Then one night when I stopped by the rooming house she told me about a man who'd had lunch there several times in the past week.

"Mac is different," she said. "Friendly, talkative, with quite a vocabulary. He likes my 'pleasant efficiency.' He's probably a grad student. At least that's what I thought at first. Then he drove off in his taxi, so I don't know."

"Is he good-looking? C'mon, don't leave out the most important part," I teased.

"Yes," she hesitated, "but in a different way. He has dark hair, combed neatly, and horn-rimmed glasses. Oh—and a thick mustache—I love the mustache—and he's serious and thoughtful."

It puzzled our family that Mac and Helen had taken to each other. Dad, ever the skeptic, seemed not so much struck with Mac's apparent education, or even with the young man's father being a professor of Latin and Greek, as he was with Mac's lowly occupation of taxi driver.

"But he's a hard worker," he told Mother, "and his influence will help Helen to settle down."

To Helen he said, "I haven't heard him speak one word about the future. It's always the past. He's twenty-six years old. He should be looking ahead to a better job."

Helen shrugged, "There's good money driving a cab in this town." She turned and walked away.

It was true that Mac seemed to live in the past, a lurid, incredible past. In the few months we had known him we'd heard about one after another of his outrageous exploits. And we were all beginning to doubt the veracity of his accounts.

"I've had some pretty close calls," he began one evening when my husband and I had dropped into the rooming house. Mac settled into an easy chair and lit his pipe. "I did some hitch-hiking a few years ago, in '36, that took me to the lumber camps in Oregon. You find tough men in a lumber camp, men that match the trees." He looked skyward, and then to us.

"Let's hear about it," I said, knowing that we *would* hear about it whether I encouraged him or not.

"They took me on, hired me to wield an ax to cut the initial wedge before the saws took over. By the end of the first week I was faster than the fellow I was paired up with." He sucked on his pipe and exhaled the fragrant smoke. "That meant trouble.

The guy was a jealous son-of-a-gun. Sometimes I found him looking at me in a way, well, in a way that made me damned uneasy. I began to ask myself, 'Are you going to kill him first, or are you going to let him bring that ax down on you?'"

Mac stared into the distance. We waited.

"Then I thought, Why let it come to that? I still had bad memories of that fellow—that scab I told you about—that I killed in the foundry workers' strike in Chicago. I didn't need anything else like that. I went into town that night and just kept going."

Dad cleared his throat and shifted in his chair.

Mother said, "You've squeezed a lot into your young life."

Helen picked up her jacket and announced, "Gotto be off to work."

My husband whispered, "Is this guy for real?" Yet we were both fascinated by him. We'd taken special note of the black leather case of medical instruments that Mac often opened and fingered.

"Sometime you'll have to tell us about your experiences with the scalpels and syringes," I said, hurrying to add, "but not tonight."

When Helen told us that she and Mac were going to be married, I asked why.

The question caught her off guard.

"It's just that neither of you seems to be in love."

Helen tossed her head and said irritably. "We get along. Don't worry about it."

Helen's marriage, that is, the ceremony, would be a first for our family. I had disappointed everyone when I was married three years before in the courthouse during a lunch break. Ironically, Helen would tie the knot properly.

February 4, 1940 was a mild hazy winter day typical of southern Wisconsin. Our family and a few friends gathered in the chapel of the Episcopalian Church, the church of Mac's father. I sat there with my husband, wondering if marriage ever lived up to its promise. Then, to strains of organ music, the bride and groom walked unescorted down the isle, Helen in a pale blue street-length dress and a clinging satin hat with a veil, Mac dignified in a dark suit. After a short ceremony everyone walked the few blocks to our parents' home.

Mother's cleaning had given a luster to our drab living room. As the guests shuffled about Mac lost no time in uncorking the champagne. Someone called for a toast "to many years of happiness" and the glasses clicked.

"My girl," Mac said with pride and affection. "'Till death do us part.' You promised, honey." He pulled her to him and brushed her lips with a kiss.

Dad seemed uneasy with Helen's and Mac's friends whom he hadn't met until now. Shifting his eyes and clearing his throat, he seemed to feel out of place at his own daughter's reception. My husband thought his social obligation was fulfilled by just attending the wedding; he went to the library after that. Mother's antennae were picking up everyone's needs as she repeated, "Yes, I'm very happy for them."

Whenever I looked at Betty her eyes were settled on Mac. I smiled a lot until my face must've looked like the taut-skinned features of a centuries old cadaver I'd seen in the museum. And the little I said seemed not quite right. I was soon to give birth to our first child, and my marriage was not what I'd hoped it would be. On this day I probably would not have been in a celebratory mood at any wedding.

The cake was three-tiered and frosted with sweeping mounds of white fluff in which two red roses were imbedded. Helen cut into it with the expertise of a good waitress. Immediately I inhaled a whiff of stale cigarettes. I traced the odor to the frosting and puzzled how it could be. No one else seemed to notice, and I said nothing. It seemed to me a fitting touch to an occasion that was not particularly festive.

Mac spoke confidently of the future. "We both have jobs. We have a nice little apartment. What about it, Helen?" He put his arm around her waist. She looked up at him and nodded in agreement.

Mother put her arms around Helen and kissed her cheek. Looking fondly at Mac, she embraced him. She liked this son-in-law. As Dad often pointed out, it was one of Mother's feminine weaknesses to see the good in people.

Helen and Mac were married less than two years when the Japanese attacked Pearl Harbor. Mac's reserve status ended abruptly. He was assigned to a base in Southern California. When they broke the news to Mother, she burst into tears and hugged them both.

"It's life," Helen said with a shrug.

As Mac and Mother talked about the implications of this momentous change, Helen shifted impatiently. "Let's get going. We've a lot to do."

From Los Angeles, Helen received an almost daily letter from Mac. Several onion-skin sheets typed and single-spaced would begin, "My darling, darling Helen," followed by a diary-like account of the day's events. While it seemed that no trivia were excluded, there was always an unexpected highlight, such as a chance meeting with a world famous dignitary. Helen would read without comment, often putting the letters aside unfinished. Mother was always eager for news from Mac. When Helen shared the letters with me, I thought how much they sounded like Mac had in our parents' living room spinning stories.

A few months passed before Helen joined him in Los Angeles. Within a week of her arrival there she wrote home, "Life is just plain boring here. Mac's gone all day, and when he's here all he wants to do is talk. But things will look up as soon as I get a job. And that won't be hard to do. This town is booming."

It was not until much later that we learned from Betty, who had also responded to the war with a westward move, that Helen and Mac had separated several times and that he had been granted a divorce in Las Vegas in September 1943. Then came the fateful day when he shipped out for the South Pacific. Betty wrote to him occasionally, to let him know someone cared, she said. Then the telegram came in the spring of '45, delivered to Betty. Mac had been killed on Okinawa.

- Chapter 10 -

Helen found life in wartime Los Angeles hectic and exciting. The feverish city bustled with newly arrived workers in the defense industries; men and women in uniform were seen everywhere. Betty, after migrating west, worked the night shift riveting the wings of airplanes at Lockheed's huge plant. Helen was swept along in the city's frenetic motion. When she wasn't waitressing she was meeting new friends over a drink in a neighborhood bar. Although it didn't take the war to impart a lusty abandon to her life, now she considered the consequences even less than before.

She could never recall how it happened that on this particular Saturday night she was in the card room back of the bar at Lucy's Den on Figueroa. Gambling was simply not her forte. Odors of beer and bourbon infiltrated the cigarette smoke and hung heavy over the crowded room. Through whiskey-numbed senses she heard a voice say, "Your play, Helen". But she felt something was wrong. The room seemed to be closing in on her. "Hell, I'm getting out of here." But before she had taken a step the crescendo of sirens panicked the roomful of gamblers. There was no exit except into the arms of the Los Angeles police.

Betty was the only one in the family to know of her whereabouts for the next half year. As soon as Helen was released from the women's prison in the Tehachapi mountains of southern California she wrote to Betty. "My six months are up. I'm out and free. I've had enough of LA. I'm heading for Frisco as soon as I say good-bye to a few friends here.

"Now I can tell you that it wasn't all typing classes, calisthenics, and boredom. I discovered that lesbian sex is good too (What else was there?). We would rendezvous in the gym with volleyball as our cover. The guards would tire of watching us and would wander off. Little Lisa would start things off. She'd go down on all of us. Then she'd look around and say, 'Now who's going to go down on little Lisa?' I'll never forget that girl. Just thought you'd like to know the realities of prison life. More will follow when I see you.

"And, Betty, I really do appreciate your helping me keep this whole mess a secret from Mom and Dad. Love, Helen."

She was unfamiliar with San Francisco's night places. Every club was popular if one could judge by the number of patrons. Why she chose the Red Lobster Inn she'd never know. The last thing she needed now—ten days out of Tehachapi—was to tangle with the police. But, tough shit. When a cop mistook her for a prostitute and started to pull her out to the street she cussed him out and tried to jerk herself free of his grip. At the same time she grabbed the arm of a young sailor and protested to the policeman, "Can't you see I'm with my boyfriend? And for Chris' sake he's shipping out tomorrow." She drew herself close to the boy as the cop loosened his grip. The sailor played the part she'd picked for him so well that the cop muttered, "Don't let me see you alone around here," and wandered off.

"Well, are you a prostitute?" the sailor asked her, amused at the unexpected role she'd foisted on him.

She let go of her hold on him. "Hell, no, I'm a waitress; I make good tips and I don't mix sex and money."

He was a lad, maybe still in his teens, sandy-haired, in bell-bottom trousers and midday blouse, with a shy smile.

"Let's have a drink." She winked and nudged him toward the bar.

They ordered martinis and he asked, "Where are you working?"

"I just came up from LA yesterday, haven't looked around much yet. It won't be a problem. I'm a good waitress, never had trouble getting a job."

They found a little table and settled into getting acquainted. After two martinis Helen reminded herself that for six months she hadn't had a drink. Better go easy. "Could we take a little walk? The Embarcadero's new to me. How about sight-seeing?"

Holding her hand he maneuvered them through the crowd and onto the street. They strolled along the waterfront and eventually to the economy-class hotel where Helen had a room. "Why don't you come up? It's early."

He hesitated.

"Look, honey, I've been in a convent for the past six months. And it'd just be nice to have a man's company for a little while." She laughed, "I'll bet you don't believe that about the convent."

He looked at her with the open-faced seriousness of a youngster and took her hands in his. "I don't care where you've been." Then very solemnly, "You were almost right when you told that cop that I ship out tomorrow. It's really day after tomorrow, but tonight's my last free night."

Hand in hand they walked into the hotel.

They spent the next day together, too. Mid afternoon found them sitting side by side in a small restaurant overlooking the Bay.

"You're a sweet girl," he said, "not at all like you seemed when that cop grabbed you last night. I don't want to remember you that way. You're not that hard girl. But, damn, I guess the war affects people in strange ways."

Contrite, the injured princess offered no defense. To herself she said, "I could be sitting in jail right now if it weren't for you."

He studied her with a quizzical expression. Abruptly he kissed her and drew her to him. "I love you. That's all I know. I love you." He released her and looked sadly into the distance as if he knew that circumstances as well as something about Helen made his hold on her very flimsy.

"Tomorrow I ship out," he said wistfully. "I'll miss you, darling. I'll miss you very much."

She took his hand and pressed her cheek against his as she gazed out over the Bay.

That night, alone in her hotel room, she felt an overwhelming loneliness. A loneliness that did not tempt her to find relief in picking up another man. She paced about the drab quarters and wept. She felt, in fact, desperate—until her eyes fastened on the razor on the dresser. Through the blur of tears she picked it up and quickly drew it through the bulging blue lines on her left wrist. With the copious flow of blood she stopped crying, wrapped a towel about the wounded wrist, and went down to the street to hail a cab for San Francisco General.

"Why did you do it?" the emergency room doctor asked.

"Don't bother me with your goddamned questions. Put a Bandaid on it and let me get the hell out of here." Her cheeks were streaked with tears as she looked at the blood-soaked towel.

She could still hear the sailor's voice, You're not that hard girl, and I love you.

As she'd told the sailor, getting a job was no problem. She was hired as a waitress by the Emerald Hotel near Union Square. With a clientele of middle class tourists it lacked the excitement of the waterfront; but no place in San Francisco was dull in 1943.

It was here, only a week after she started to work, that she met John. She was immediately attracted to him, a tall, well-built, self-assured man. But she found something about him intimidating. Her flirtations were usually playful and fleeting. Now she had the uneasy feeling that she was potential prey. He had the steel blue eyes of our father. And she had learned how to handle Daddy. Her initial premonitions vanished when he turned on his charm.

He asked her if she'd like to see a play with him. *Dark of the Moon* was playing at the Orpheum. She told him, "I don't date customers."

"Who do you date?"

"I don't discuss my personal life with people who dine here."

For the next three days she served him breakfast and dinner in a no-nonsense manner. She hoped it concealed her interest in him.

He told her the essentials of his current existence. He was forty-one-years-old and had a little business in Henderson, Nevada, a town of about 3,000 population before the war. Now the place bustled with the activities of an army ordnance depot. He came to the city every few months to escape the pervasive sand and heat and boredom of the desert.

His fourth day at the Emerald was Helen's day off. He encountered her alone at the corner of Van Ness and O'Farrell, near Tommy's Place, about nine o'clock in the evening.

"My dear Helen, how fortunate that I should meet you tonight, just before I'm to leave. Come, have a drink with me." He took her arm. "Let's get acquainted. You must have surmised that I am very attracted to you."

John was a man with a suavity she was not accustomed to. He wooed her ardently and assured her, "It is destiny, my dear girl, that has brought us together."

She succumbed.

He extended his stay.

Within the week, a phone call from Betty in Wisconsin urged her to come home. Mother had just been hospitalized with congestive heart failure and was not expected to recover.

She left the next day, but not before John had extracted from her a promise that her return to the West would be, not to San Francisco, but to Henderson, Nevada.

In Wisconsin she stayed with me for a few weeks while she visited our mother. She felt at loose ends and told us nothing of John. When it became apparent that Mother's illness would be prolonged, Helen took a train West.

On her return to John in Nevada he surprised her with gifts more elegant than anything she had known. "For my princess," he said, clasping her face in his hands and kissing her. Flustered, she stroked the fur and gazed long at the jade.

"John, honey," she said, affection shining from her eyes, we hardly know each other. You shouldn't have . . ." She put both arms about him and snuggled her face against his neck.

"Tonight, my dear, we're going to celebrate your return to me in Las Vegas."

"It'll be a first for me," she said expectantly.

They were one of many expensively-dressed couples in the casino. He, urbane and charming. She, lovely with her auburn hair pulled softly back into a bun low on her aristocratic neck. Jade dangled from her ears and a mink stole covered her shoulders. They sat in the cocktail lounge with drinks. She was not comfortable in this milieu of rich gamblers. She sipped her drink and frowned. "John, honey, when I order a Manhattan I expect some whiskey in it. Call that waiter and . . ."

"Helen, don't throw your weight around in this place. I don't want us to be conspicuous. Drink your Manhattan," he said with the firmness of a strict father.

"Well, if you won't take care of me . . ." she raised her hand to signal the waiter.

With swiftness and strength that frightened her John seized her arm and held it to the table. It might have appeared an innocent move to an onlooker, but to Helen it was a clear warning that this was a man she'd best not trifle with.

"You like to wear jade and furs? They're yours, baby, if you use your head. You're a beautiful woman; we can make a great team. But I won't take that kind of behavior from you. You could do with a little sophistication."

Quick to understand, Helen concealed her surprise and anger and said sarcastically, "OK, darling, I can see that I'm to become a clever woman with your help."

- Chapter 11 -

It was almost a year later, in August, 1944 that Helen wrote to Mother. "Don't scold me for not writing sooner. I do hope you are feeling better, Mother. I'm here in Henderson with John, a business-man I met in Frisco.

"The heat is unbearable. We did well until recently when the Army units began to leave. Now the place is deserted. I was laid off, and John's business is terrible. I've been having a lot of lower abdominal pain. The doc thinks it's my tubes and uterus. Sure hope I don't have to have surgery. Tell Kay I hope school is going well. Next time you hear from me it'll probably be from a different place. Love, Helen."

The letter addressed to our mother was returned, stamped "Deceased." Helen had been notified by telegram five days earlier. Now she sat staring at the letter, and cried.

Mother's last year had been spent in a hospital. During the first months that Dad was alone he wrote several times to Helen. Now she took his letters from a drawer and reread them. The last letter was dated December 10, 1943. "Dear Helen, I have been alone now since Mother went into the hospital. I take the bus to see her twice a week. Feeling as I do I never know whether each day will be the last for me. I want you to know that my mind is with you all the time. With my love for you as strong as ever, little Helen, Dad."

One day in early January, when the neighbors did not see him sitting as usual in the front window with the newspaper and his morning coffee, they investigated and found his body on the kitchen floor, his broken coffee cup beside him.

Tears had always come easily to Helen, as had laughter. Now as she thought of Dad, as well as of Mother, she could not stop the flow.

She and John joined the exodus from Henderson. He told her about a lucrative business he'd had some years ago in Akron, Ohio. He still had connections there, and it was just possible that they could make a mint in that city. It sounded good to Helen. They headed into the unknown of Ohio. When financial success eluded John and nothing seemed to be working out for them, he insisted that Helen help out—beyond her wages from waitress work. Taking his advice she opened her own checking account at a bank.

At John's insistence ("people trust you," he said) she wrote and cashed several large checks not covered by money in her account. With the cash in hand they lost no time leaving Ohio. They flew to Las Vegas. "With this we can win a lot more," he said confidently. During a day and a night in Vegas they won nothing, and consoled themselves that their losses were negligible.

"Dear, it would be prudent for us to depart Las Vegas soon, meaning now. I already have tickets for the city that's your favorite as well as mine."

In San Francisco, John made the unexpected announcement that he wanted to legitimate their relationship. They had never discussed marriage. But, in her present danger, his proposal had the effect of magnifying his role of protector, and decreased her fears that the police would soon catch up with her. They were married August 27, 1945 and moved into a modest apartment near the marina. Within the week, Helen felt so restless that she went out and got a job in a nearby restaurant.

"John, honey, I can't just sit around. And my skin doesn't take well to hours of lying on the beach."

Meanwhile, the Ohio authorities were not idle. According to the Akron Daily News, ". . . detectives made two cross-country trips totaling 7,000 miles to Las Vegas and San Francisco to return the twenty-seven-year-old woman on the charge of issuing checks without funds."

Again, letters from prison. This time from the State Reformatory at Marysville, Ohio. "Dear Betty, I'm being 'rehabilitated.' Trained as a dietician's assistant. They thought that since all I'd done was waitress work I could advance into this. In a year I'll be eligible for parole. I'm sure I'll make it. Everybody likes me. I'm a model inmate. Really. Love, Helen."

On her release she was paroled to Orlando, Florida, where John now resided. She worked as a dietician's assistant in the Orlando Tuberculosis Sanitarium. Living with John again was not easy. He was sullen and grumpy much of the time. She studied him now as they sat in the living room with their drinks. He was a far call from the smooth businessman she'd met at the Emerald Hotel, slouched in his chair, half a dozen cigarette butts in the ash tray.

"John, you're not happy. Maybe we should get out more. Sitting here every evening is pretty boring."

"Your leaving me alone for the past year hasn't helped."

"What do you mean, 'I left you?' They took me!" No point reminding him that it was at his urging she'd written the checks. That would only lead to another fight. And they were getting ugly.

"Yeah, it is boring," he said, pushing himself out of the chair with effort. "Let's go for a walk at the lake."

She put out her cigarette, pulled on sandals and walked into the dusk with him. Above the horizon strands of pink and purple stretched across the sky and were reflected on the still surface of the lake. She reached for his hand; he pulled it away. When they came to a bench they sat and watched the water lap at the sand.

"You want to know one reason I'm not in a good mood these

days?" he asked. "Renovating lakeshore cabins is hardly a job I'm cut out for. Worse, it'll end one of these days, and I've no idea what I'll find then."

"We're getting by all right. And we're together again."

A couple strolled past arm in arm. Ten feet out a fish arced into the air. The fading sunset left the sky to the stars. As they started to walk toward home their movement muffled the rhythmic sound of the water at their feet.

After a long silence he said, "Do you ever think about that incident in Georgia? Suppose they'll ever connect you with it?"

"Why should they? All my I.D.s were in a different name. Why do you bring it up? Does someone know?"

They walked a little farther before he said, "I'm the only one who knows. Maybe you ought to think about that."

At home in bed he pulled her to him, as if daring her to resist, kissed her with cold wet lips, entered her, and in a few strokes, climaxed. She got up, went to the kitchen and poured herself a drink.

The next day she phoned Betty. "The tension between us is getting unbearable. Please come visit. I need help to sort things out and decide what to do. Don't worry, he'll be hospitable."

On her arrival, John was indeed hospitable, almost charming. "Here, take this comfortable chair. See, it affords you a view of our magnolia tree . . . What would you like to drink? I can mix anything you can name."

"No alcohol. Coffee would be good."

The next day when Helen came home from work, Betty was resting in the guest room. John was muttering angrily in the kitchen.

Helen saw the contents of the cupboards thrown about onto the counters and the floor. She shrieked, "What the hell's the problem?"

"The problem," he said through clenched teeth, "is that you're not taking care of this house the way you should. And I won't tolerate this chaos any longer."

Helen had just put in an eight-hour day at the sanitarium. She looked at him scornfully and reached over the piles of cans, boxes, and bags for the bottle of bourbon. But he grabbed it first. She backed toward the door. Livid, he pitched the bottle at her. She screamed as it grazed the top of her head, and looked desperately for a way to defend herself. She snatched a half-empty jar of dill pickles and flung it wildly at him. He caught it with a mean laugh.

"Well, my darling, you're living in my house now. When will you learn that I'm running this show?" He moved closer to her. "You don't give in gracefully."

She sobbed, unnerved.

"Now be a good girl," he taunted, pulling her into his arms. "You just need to get a few things straight."

Betty was clearly worried. "Helen, he's a dangerous man. He could kill you."

"I've gone along with him on everything. And what did I get for it? Prison. And now this."

"I'll go with you tomorrow to see your parole officer. You can't live in this house with him any longer."

They convinced her parole officer to allow her to live in the sanitarium where she worked.

John was not about to let her off so easily. He wrote to her, "Helen—I'm giving you a choice between coming home and being the sweet girl I love or going to jail for a period of years, probably with no chance of parole. It's for you to decide. I expect a reply no later than next Tuesday.

"I talked to your parole officer and learned that you had spent Wednesday night away from the hospital and had not come in to work Thursday morning. He will report it to the Ohio authorities. He doesn't know about that other case yet. And whether he does depends on you. He said you told him you were through with me. Well, you're not through with me and you won't be for a long time to come. I want you to sign over the ring to me in case you're taken out of state. What is your answer? John."

Upon receipt of the letter, Helen conferred with her parole officer. He concurred that she was not safe in the same city with

John. The Ohio authorities agreed to let her live in San Francisco with an older woman friend whom they investigated and found to be reliable. Before the deadline John had given her she secretly left Orlando.

A few months later her San Francisco parole officer informed her that John had been granted a divorce. That was good. Now the ring was all that remained between them. Dazzlingly beautiful, it was a solitary ruby set in a crown of gold. She was selective about when and where she wore it. Most of the time it was secreted in a little velvet-covered box.

Finally, her parole came to an end. Betty flew up from Los Angeles to help her celebrate. She took a room at the St Francis Hotel and invited Helen to spend the night there with her. When she arrived, the ring conspicuously adorned the fourth finger of her right hand. After dinner they went to the cocktail lounge on the top floor of the hotel. Helen had seemed happy until, after too many whiskies on the rocks, she became maudlin. "The bastard damned near ruined my life. I'll never be safe anyplace."

Betty tried to calm her. "You said your P.O. thought the divorce would take care of everything, and that John wouldn't harass you."

"There's just one thing between that son-of-a-bitch and me. And that's this ring."

She gazed at it and held her hand where the candlelight enhanced its beauty. Betty got up and took Helen's arm. "Let's go down to my room. One drink was enough for me, and you'll feel better tomorrow if you stop now."

Helen wiped the tears from her face and smiled in agreement. She pushed back her chair and walked unsteadily with Betty to the elevator.

In Betty's room, Helen sank into a chair. "Betty, you've been with me through so much trouble; I could always trust you." With those words she burst into sobs. As Betty sat on the edge of the chair with her arm on her shoulder, Helen began to study the ring on her right fourth finger. She slid it off, and then back on. Finally, she stood up and walked about the room. She stopped before the window and stared down to the street seven floors below. She took the ring from her finger, fondled it for a few seconds, then dropped it out of the window.

"I just released the last claim the son-of-a-bitch has on me. Let's go to bed. I'm tired."

In a bar on Sutter Street she met Vic, an army sergeant. Good-looking, stocky build, jovial and crude, he appealed to her in an impulsive comfortable way. They had a few dates. He was about to be transferred to a base in Oklahoma. She went with him.

"Vic, honey, it's hell being a waitress in this place. With this humidity, the heat's worse than Nevada."

But in October 1950, when the Question Man in the Enid, Oklahoma Sunday newspaper asked eight waitresses, "What kind of service brings the best tips?" Helen's picture was that of a snappy smiling woman. Any reader would bet on her knowing how to rake in the tips.

Vic brought word of his impending transfer to a base near Fresno.

Helen was disheartened. "Honey, can't the Army do better than this? Enid? Now that inferno Fresno?"

"You don't have to come along, baby," he teased.

But by now they were married, it would take more than disagreeable weather to keep her from him.

- Chapter 12 -

"Helen, it's over. Do you want to get the divorce or shall I?"

She'd expected this pronouncement from Vic. Without looking up from her nails she was manicuring, she said, "I can't be bothered."

There was nothing else to be settled between them. All they owned was in the dresser drawers and clothes closets of the little house they rented near the World War II Army Air Force base. He paced about the sparsely furnished house as if expecting an argument, then poured himself a drink and settled down at the kitchen table.

She slipped out of her waitress uniform, showered, and applied fresh make-up. Then she confronted the wardrobe closet, the only congested part of the house. Separating the hangers of tightly squeezed clothing, she paused, considered, and chose a stunning blue-gray knit dress. After an approving glance in the mirror she stepped into the cool evening air of California's Central Valley. Half a block away was the Crossroads Tavern.

She pushed the door open and paused to survey the familiar scene. Her eyes settled on a stranger at the bar, a tall well-built fellow with a suntanned face beneath a shock of graying hair, far and away the best looking man in the room. She walked directly to the empty stool beside him. Beckoning the bar-tender, she ordered, "Bourbon, straight".

She felt the stranger's eyes scanning her. She enjoyed attracting men. Tonight, in the clinging blue wool and her defiant mood she was ready for whatever the night might bring.

He leaned toward her. "Problems, baby?"

Hearing no impertinence in his query, she glanced at him and smiled.

"You looked like an unhappy angel as you stood by that door. I can see that somebody's clipped your wings."

She said nothing as he emptied his glass and looked thoughtfully at the counter. She reached for the bourbon the bartender had set before her.

"That's no drink for a woman," he counseled. "Hard on the throat. Let me buy you . . . what?"

She winked at the bartender as she compromised. "Make it on the rocks."

They carried their glasses to a corner table.

"I haven't seen you here before," she said.

"My name's Tom. I don't often get this far from my home base of San Jose."

"This is a godforsaken place," she said. "Hot as hell in the summer and fog that chills your bones in the winter. I wouldn't be here except that I was stupid enough to marry a sergeant in the Army. But that's ending." She tilted her chin up, then pulled a cigarette from a pack in her purse. "Better late than never. You married?"

"Yeah. She works at the Moffitt Air Field. I don't see much of her. We got no problems, just seldom see each other. And there's nothing wrong with that . . . Eh, honey, how about another drink?"

They drank and talked long into the night.

When she turned in her uniform the next morning, that valley town lost its best waitress. She packed her clothes and stuffed her belongings into Tom's station wagon.

"San Jose needs waitresses, too, doll," he encouraged. "In

fact, I know a place."

Helen found a two-room apartment in the northeast part of the city among low-income working people like herself. On the day that she moved in, she discovered, only half a block away a bar called The Derby. By nightfall she and Tom had met most of her new neighbors over a drink.

Seldom a day passed without her seeing Tom. His work, selling pumps and well equipment to area farmers, often took him away from home. And when Helen wasn't working she was with him, usually waiting over a drink at a country tavern while he was demonstrating a product.

Her apartment was merely a place to hang her clothes and to sleep. Like the house in the Valley, it was not for living. When they weren't traveling or at the Derby, they were at his house, an isolated and neglected place at the edge of town. Helen knew from the beginning that Tom lived with his wife. Ethel's life fit well with theirs. She worked at the air field thirty miles from town, usually daytimes, occasionally the swing shift. Helen adjusted her own hours, and sometimes her jobs, to be with Tom when his wife wasn't home. She did her laundry there, prepared meals from supplies in the cupboards, watched TV in the living room, and shared with Tom the only bed in the house. He did not seem uneasy with this arrangement, and taking her cue from him, neither was Helen. If his wife divorced him he risked losing the house, he explained to Helen. And, after years of paying on a mortgage, he preferred to hold onto the house. That was the only reason he ever gave for continuing the marriage.

Helen was becoming increasingly comfortable among his wife's possessions. She used uncharacteristic discretion, never borrowing anything Ethel was likely to miss. She used her perfume at Tom's request so as not to introduce new scents into the house. And when she wore Ethel's clothes she took pains to return them to the closet the same day. Thus month after month, and year after year passed without a confrontation between Helen and Ethel or between Ethel and Tom.

Helen looked at her watch and sighed, "I shouldn't dally. It's time for me to go." It was a September afternoon in the late '50s. Tom gave her no argument. She slipped out from between the bed sheets and reached for her clothes. As she stepped into her aqua-colored uniform she said, "I practically live in my uniform. I haven't bought anything new in months . . . Hey, what's this?" She was browsing through Ethel's wardrobe. "Honey, what's Ethel doing with an outfit like this?" She whistled in awe as she held before her a flame-colored satin gown with floor-length flared trousers.

"I mean it, honey, I can't imagine Ethel wearing this."

"She'll probably wear it to the Christmas party at the base," he said without apparent interest. "I never go to those affairs. And she doesn't mind. In fact, she says she has more fun without me."

Helen was transfixed by visions of herself in this sparkling gown. As her mind came back to the room she snapped her fingers to announce, "The first Saturday she works I'll wear it." She could see herself entering the Derby in red satin. "You know, I looked up my name in the dictionary once. Helen means flame or torch. So, what's more appropriate than this?" She stepped into the wide flared trousers, then pulled on the sleeveless sequined blouse. Tom pressed her to him, caressing her silky smooth buttocks. "I like you in this, baby. Shall I buy you one like it?"

"Hell, no. It won't hurt her to share."

She waited only until the second week-end to execute her plan. Ethel was to work overtime that week. As his wife told Tom, "I can't pass up a chance to earn a little extra, because you hardly make enough these days to cover the mortgage."

By seven o'clock on Saturday night most of the men who hung out at the Derby had changed into clean clothes, and their wives had finished the dishes and arranged for the care of the children. Helen often baby-sat somebody's youngsters when Tom couldn't be with her. But tonight Tom would be here. She had been at his house an hour ago to pick up the dress.

When the Saturday night crowd filled the tavern Helen swept across the room, Tom close behind her, to whistles and applause.

People flocked about her. Slowly, after a flurry of exclamations and compliments, they wandered back to their earlier conversations.

Joanie and Shortie remained. "Tom bought it for you?" Joanie asked.

"It's his wife's," Helen boasted. "It just hangs in the closet. She never wears it."

Joanie looked troubled.

At about ten o'clock, Shortie announced that he would dash home to see if their kids were all right. Seconds after he opened the door to leave the Derby, he bounded back and virtually fell into Helen and Tom. "It's Ethel. She's parking across the street."

He grabbed Helen and pushed her ahead of him into the utility room behind the bar.

Helen was furious. "The bitch. How'd she know that Tom was here?"

"I'll work things out with Tom. You get home and change. I'll be at your place in a few minutes." Shortie returned to the crowd and was immediately face to face with Ethel.

"Nice to see you, Ethel. Tom drinks alone too much."

"Tom drinks too much, period," his wife said dryly.

"Well, I've got to run home and check on the kids, then do a little errand across town, and I'll be right back." He held Tom's eyes long enough to be sure the message had registered. "Hope you folks'll be here when I get back."

"Damn right, we'll be here," Ethel said. "Tom hasn't taken me out in months. When I found out the last minute that I didn't have to work tonight, I said to myself, I'll track that man down and we'll have a night out."

Helen left the Derby by the back door and walked half a block to her duplex. There she took a last admiring look at herself in the full length mirror on the closet wall. "Bitch," she whispered. Then she looked through her wardrobe. There was nothing as attention getting as the red satin outfit. She put on a simple black sheath, adorned only by a shiny ten-inch fringe that hung from the hem to just below the knees, permitting glimpses of her thighs through the dangling strands. It was a dress that brought more than the usual comments about her beautiful legs. She selected from the jewelry box an imitation jade necklace and matching earrings.

Shortie was at the door to drive her to Tom and Ethel's house to return the gown. "How're you going to get in?"

"With my key, stupid," she laughed smugly.

Fifteen minutes later the gown was back in its owner's closet with no hint that it had ever been elsewhere.

As they returned to the vicinity of the Derby, Shortie became apprehensive. "I think I should take you home."

"Hell no, you don't."

They entered the Derby separately, she pouting and hesitating on each step.

"Hey, Helen, where's your man tonight?" Joe called out.

"Men who drink too much should keep their mouths shut," she snapped.

As Helen elbowed her way to the bar, someone whispered in her ear, "Darling, you're prettier in red."

"Leave me alone," she said petulantly to everyone who approached her. Sulking, she leaned against the bar.

"Who's that woman?" Ethel asked.

"Just a gal lives up the street," Shortie answered casually.

"She sure knows how to get attention," Ethel observed.

"Seems like something went wrong for her tonight," Shortie said with a grin.

- Chapter 13 -

"This damn tumor won't hold still," Helen wrote in a letter
to me the following spring. "It's grown further into the right side
of my throat. Hurts like hell. They're going to operate again. Dr.
C. says there's a good possibility they can remove all of the new
growth. And if they do perhaps they can go ahead with the skin
grafting. I've become attached (pun) to this roll on my chest. But
I'd sure like to get rid of it.

"I'll be going into the hospital next Sunday. Wait a few days
before you visit me since I'll be uncomfortable at first. Love,
Helen."

Uncomfortable? What an understatement! As a small child I
had suffered through one sore throat after another every winter.
Every attempt to swallow or to speak aggravated the pain for
which there was no relief. I'd curl up in bed, turn to the wall
feigning sleep, and pray that my parents wouldn't come to feel
my forehead and ask how I felt. Now I winced at the thought of
Helen's cancerous throat being further carved away.

Daily phone calls to the Intensive Care Unit assured me that
Helen was recovering without any unexpected problems. Six
days after the operation Betty and I drove to San Jose to visit her.
We were silent as the odometer registered the passing miles. My

thoughts were on Helen and I feared that any comment I might make about our sister would elicit disagreement from Betty. I wanted to be considerate of Betty's spiritual beliefs, and was stuck in thinking about the physical aspects of Helen's illness. Perhaps Betty was silent for a similar reason or, more likely, because it was Betty's nature to keep her thoughts to herself. Finally I couldn't bear the quiet. "I can't help wondering how I would cope with a situation like Helen's. I don't think I would be able to go through all this."

Betty said nothing.

I was the one who had chosen to confront illness and suffering in others as a career. But my years of experience had given only superficial understanding. "Don't you agree that Helen seemed headed for disaster almost from the beginning?"

Betty hesitated. "Prayer and faith could take her in a different direction, even now." Both my medical and Betty's metaphysical considerations were inadequate and I'd come to regard illness simply as part of the human condition.

Finally Betty said, "Suffering and sickness are illusions."

And I, without taking my eyes off the road, imagined in my sister's deep gray eyes a mysterious, all-knowing expression. I recalled, without reminding Betty, that she had not always considered the physical body to be an illusion. Throughout her childhood, the bulbous birthmark on her upper lip had been so painfully real that she spent the first money she earned after high school for plastic surgery to repair the deformity.

Although I rejected many of Betty's mystical beliefs, the New Age influences of the early '70s had led me to be curious about her convictions. Dreams, telepathy, and synchronicity fascinated me. Only a few weeks ago I'd spent an evening with a friend discussing the possibility of my working in Africa. He'd shown me pictures he'd taken there. The next morning my son said, "Mom, last night I dreamed there were elephants and lions in our yard."

A couple of years ago Betty's husband died in my home. When I left for work in the morning, he was doing what he loved—pruning my roses. I returned late afternoon to find him lying lifeless on the couch, the serenity of his face suggesting a vision of bliss. (He had had a heart attack.) In a dream a few nights later, he had become the rich earth colors and blue of the cosmos. I could no longer feel sure that death was the end.

But now, as we were about to visit Helen in her worsening condition, was not a propitious time for me to attempt a reconciliation of our beliefs. I would become exasperated because hers are rigidly entrenched while mine are nebulous, formative.

"I know it's important for us to visit Helen," Betty said, "but I hate hospitals. I feel so strongly that true healing is spiritual. I said that to Helen one day, and she just blinked those blue eyes and stared at me. When she turned away it was obvious she didn't want to hear more."

"I'm probably as uncomfortable in hospitals as you are," I said. "I resent the arrogance that seems to be built into these institutions. So much of the pleasantness is phony. There's not enough real caring. I'm afraid that medical treatment focuses on diseases rather than on people."

We pulled into the visitors' parking lot at Valley Memorial Hospital and took the now familiar trek to the elevator in the lobby. When we walked into Helen's room on the surgical ward we found her sitting up in bed watching TV. She waved a greeting and motioned us to turn it off and sit down. She wasn't interested in the stupid show, she gestured. Betty and I stood beside the bed. A naso-gastric tube was plastered with white tape against Helen's forehead, and bulky white bandages encircled her neck. Her pallor, above a pink satin robe gave her a soft attractive vulnerability. But for only a moment. The image changed as she energetically thrust out her hand for a pencil and wrote an account of the surgery.

"The tumor had infiltrated deeper into the neck tissues than Dr. C. expected. He had to remove muscles that I need for swallowing. That's not good. But he says it won't be as much of a problem for me as it would be for a lot of people because my attitude's so good. He's pessimistic as to whether they'll ever get to the skin grafting." She held the paper out for us to read. She took it back and continued. "He's honest with me, and he knows I value that. I couldn't feel more confidence in anyone than I do in Dr. C."

Betty, confronted with the physical reality of Helen's cancer, looked at one object after another about the small room. Then she let her eyes settle on Helen, bandaged and incubated, but still in control. "Do you realize that I'm about to graduate from Hayward State? Next month. At age 49! Who would ever have thought it possible? The kids are proud of me."

"As well they should be," I said, thinking of how little recognition Betty had had in her life.

Helen raised her hand, thumb and index finger forming a circle. Then she wrote, "Let's take a little walk. I'd like to go to the lobby."

The lobby? I was taken aback.

We took the elevator to the hospital waiting room. It was spacious, attractive, and starkly impersonal in spite of the visitors sitting about on colorful naughahide sofas under glowing lamps. Heads turned toward us: Helen, her regal bearing undiminished by tape and gauze and a week in bed; Betty, like Helen, taller than average, her square face framed by short straight hair, her movements slow, tentative; I, smaller than the other two, my manner concealing, I hoped, how truly mousy I felt at this moment.

Helen walked to the flower stand and presented the woman attendant with a note. As the lady read, "My sisters," Helen motioned proudly to Betty and me.

"She's wonderful," the flower lady told us. And to Helen, "Dearie, you look great, and so soon after surgery."

Tilting her chin, Helen winked.

At home a few days later I received a letter. "I was doing fine until I got a wound infection. They're giving me a strong antibiotic into my veins. My arm's red and swollen—phlebitis, they call it. I get narcotics above what I need for the neck pain, just to ease my aching arm. The doctor says it's coming along well. And to me it seems better. So I'm not worried."

The next message was from Joanie, a phone call from the

Derby. Tom had died last night from a heart attack.

Again Betty and I piled into my little Fiat and headed south.

At the hospital we found Helen composed but with red eyes and blotchy skin. Her lips quivered as she described on her notepad what had happened. Tom, unbeknown to her, had been brought into the intensive care unit down the hall from her room. Their mutual friends, so concerned about him and whether he would make it, didn't think to tell Helen until it was too late.

"I could've held him", she mouthed as tears overflowed her lids and she encircled the space before her with her arms.

Again her pencil: "The doctors say I won't be able to go to the funeral. Maybe it's just as well. It would make me sick to see his wife crying over him."

- **Chapter 14** -

As Betty and I drove home, assured that Helen would have the support of friends in the days ahead, I mused. "It's interesting how the three of us have come together at this time in Northern California. Remember in our childhood the family's dreams of going West?"

When hints of spring appeared in March, and Dad got restless, we'd all get caught up in the fantasy of venturing West.

"If only I could start over, I tell you, we'd be in California now. A few years ago I'd have hitched up the horses and we'd have taken off." (In the '20s, Dad was confident that the automobile was but a passing fancy.) "But it's too late now."

"Why is it too late, Daddy?"

"Well, for one thing, a few years ago we had money. Now times are hard. We'd starve before we got to Nebraska." Then, sensing our disappointment, "Maybe next spring."

Betty reminisced, "Helen was the first. She came to LA with Mac soon after they were married."

"Soon after that you surprised me by pulling up stakes."

"I surprised myself. Riveting wings on airplanes at Lockheed on a night shift. Making big money for the first time. Feeling free."

She looked into the darkness, silent for awhile. "I don't know if I ever told you," her voice secretive, "but I spent a lot of time with Mac before he shipped out. Helen had ignored him. It was as if they weren't married. And . . . the truth is, I fell in love with Mac. Helen didn't know, and she wouldn't have cared if she had known." Again she lapsed into silence.

I glanced at her and waited.

"When he was killed on Okinawa I was the one who cried. I was the one who took his belongings that the Army shipped to Helen. I took the responsibility of phoning his family in Indiana."

I pondered her revelations. "Betty, your ability to keep secrets always amazed me. I'm truly surprised and, I guess, pleased. Mac, for all his braggadocio, seemed a tragic figure to me. I'm glad you cared for him, even if I learn it thirty years late . . . But he must have meant something to Helen. She's using his name again."

A few miles further down the highway I reminded us, "The war was an opportunity for me too. I wouldn't have been admitted to medical school in any normal year. And school would have been impossible with my children only two and three years old without the War Nursery."

"The war affected each of us differently," she commented.

"It wasn't until '59 that I moved out here with my second family, Jack and the baby. You had gone back to Wisconsin. Did I ever tell you about that first Christmas in California when I invited Helen to be with us?"

I wasn't without qualms about this visit. I hadn't seen Helen for over five years and we never wrote. But my nostalgia, heightened by the season, dictated that Helen should be with us. Tom had no family obligations; Ethel always worked on Christmas day. So Helen said they'd come on Christmas Eve. My older sons would be coming from Wisconsin.

I took a few days off from work to prepare for the holidays: planning refreshments, shopping for groceries, wrapping presents, helping Jack trim the tree. We both delighted in our two-year-old's interest in the sparkle and color that decorated the house.

Christmas Eve was a joyous reunion with my older sons. But,

as the hours passed and Helen and Tom had not arrived, Jack and the boys went to bed. I sat, in nightgown and robe, waiting and wondering. Shortly after midnight the doorbell rang.

"We stopped to have a drink with Joyce and her husband. They live real near you, Kay," Helen explained.

No embrace marked this reunion. It had always been this way.

"It's my fault, Kay," Tom apologized. "I wanted Helen to meet some old friends in the Canyon. We got tied up longer than we expected."

"I wish you'd have phoned," I said with restraint. "I was sure that something had happened. You know how one always thinks of an accident."

My voice sounded wrong, angry and anxious. I searched for feelings more appropriate to the season. Thankfulness, perhaps, that they had arrived at all.

Helen's eyes moved about restlessly. I imagined her thinking, *You disapprove, tough shit. We can't all be perfect like you.*

But before Helen could speak or flounce out of the door, Tom said, "Kay must be tired with all the Christmas hassle. Kay, where do you want us to sleep? But first, a nightcap. What do you have to drink?"

I opened a cupboard and pointed to a bottle of rum and a half-empty fifth of brandy. "There's eggnog in the refrigerator and soda."

"Tom can mix something," Helen offered. "You know how I like mine, honey, with about this much water." She measured an inch between her thumb and forefinger.

"You, Kay?" Tom asked.

"Nothing, thanks. We had a couple drinks while we were waiting for you. Helen can tell you that my limit's one or two."

"Yeah," Helen said, expressing disgust as well as confirmation "That's Kay for you. But Christ, Kay, this is Christmas Eve."

We sat at the kitchen table. Tom lit a cigarette for Helen, then one for himself.

"I'll bet she hides her ash trays, honey. Don't you, Kay? No, don't get up. I'll find one." She pulled an ash tray from a top drawer.

I opened a window.

Tom relaxed. "I'm really sorry about getting here so late. I was inconsiderate of Helen, too. She's been working too much and not getting enough rest."

"You can say that again." She clasped her hand over his.

"Helen's independent; that's good. But she doesn't always take care of herself. All Joanie or Carrie have to do is ask her to babysit and she's there for them."

"I should take Tom's advice. He's good for me. Keeps me from drinking too much—except tonight." She squeezed his hand. "And keeps me from other foolish things—I won't name them."

"She hasn't been in jail, even one night, since we've been together."

"That's right," she said with pride.

Tom pulled her up from the chair and kissed her.

I showed them to the bedroom.

During the night Helen coughed unremittingly. I was in and out of bed trying to find a remedy. Helen sat up, dragging on a cigarette for relief and coughing more. Cough drops were of no help, nor were the syrups I took from the medicine cabinet. When it looked as if Helen might finally get to sleep, I said, "I'll try to keep the boys quiet in the morning so you can get some rest."

By eight o'clock everyone was up except the late night guests. Just as the boys finished opening presents Helen and Tom joined us. Then for the first time an oversight occurred to me. "Helen, I'm embarrassed. I have no gifts for you."

Helen looked at Tom. "Kay was never sentimental, even about birthdays and Christmas." To me, "You'll feel better to know that we forgot to pick up something for you, too. We're even."

"Coffee smells good," Tom said. "I need some of that."

"Warm milk with brandy's all I want," Helen said. "And some Alka Seltzer if you have any."

I started to the kitchen and motioned Helen to follow. "C'mon and visit with me while I get breakfast," I heated milk and poured the last of the brandy into it. As Helen pulled out a chair to sit down my toddler eyed her curiously.

"Here, let Aunt Helen hold you." She reached to pick him up, but he squirmed away to return to the tree, the toys, and the men folk.

I thought of our sister in Wisconsin. "I'll bet it's a mad house at Betty's now, with six little kids tearing the wrappings off presents."

"I miss seeing those little farts. You know, Kay, the regret of my life is not having had a kid. That San Francisco gynecologist said I had so many adhesions I'd never have gotten pregnant even if he hadn't taken out my uterus." She wiped a tear from her cheek. "I don't think much of gynecologists. You remember the advice Betty got when she was only eighteen? That she probably could never get pregnant?" She stopped suddenly. "Kay, I'm feeling sick. Don't you have any Alka Seltzer?"

Pale and trembling, she started toward Tom to the living room. I left the bacon frying and the coffee cake in the oven to follow. Jack was occupied with the baby. My sons cast questioning looks at me. With false cheeriness I said, "Breakfast's almost ready. You'll feel better, Helen, when you eat something."

Christmas morning was one of the happiest times of the year for me. And breakfast was an essential part of that pleasure. Breakfast with a little extra touch, with such aromas as now filled the house.

"We can't eat without Aunt Helen," one of the boys insisted.

"She's sick," I said grimly. "We're going to have to eat without Aunt Helen."

Tom and Helen had sunk onto the couch. The others came to the table reluctantly. It would have taken more than the aroma of coffee, bacon, and warm pastry, more that the red and green citrus peel on the cake to make this gathering festive.

Helen retched. "It's the sight and smell of that food," she complained as she hurried toward the bathroom.

"She'll be all right," Tom said. "There's no brandy left?"

Helen returned in a few minutes. She was dragging deeply on a cigarette, barely able to hold it in her shaking hand. "Tom, honey, do you think we could go out for a little while? Get some fresh air? Drive around a little maybe?"

"I wish I could do something," I said, knowing it would take another drink to make Helen feel better. "Come back soon so we can visit. And don't forget dinner about four." But they didn't return that day.

A week later Helen wrote, "Kay, honey, I hope you're not angry with us. But Tom had some friends. We stopped in, didn't expect to stay long, but you know how it goes sometimes. Hope you had a nice Xmas. Love, Helen."

"Yes, we've all realized the dream of living in California," I said as we neared the end of the drive home from our visit to Helen in the hospital.

- Chapter 15 -

Ten days had passed since Betty and I visited Helen in the hospital. The nurses kept us informed of her progress and relayed her messages to us.

Then I had an unexpected phone call one evening. I answered to hear Dr. Callahan's distraught voice. I had not talked to him for over a year when he'd called to discuss the possibility of complications from Helen's initial surgery.

"What's Helen up to? I can't make any sense of it," he started sharply, abruptly.

"I don't know what you're talking about", I said, suddenly on guard.

"You don't know about the suit? You don't know she's suing me?"

"Oh, no!" I was stunned. "She tells me again and again, in fact in a letter I got this morning, that she wouldn't be alive if it weren't for you. Suing you? I can't believe it. Of course I didn't know about it."

"Yes, she's suing the hospital and me for malpractice."

Dr. Callahan was a brilliant young surgeon from the University Medical Center. Helen had taken to him immediately. "My doctor," she called him with possessive pride. When she went through surgery with none of the feared complications she became a showcase for him. He brought other doctors to see her, and never failed to attribute his surgical success to her upbeat attitude.

I slowly recalled, "Many months ago she hinted of a suit against her first doctor who found the tumor and didn't do a biopsy. But she didn't speak openly of it to me. I think she knew I suspected it was her own fault a biopsy wasn't done."

"I visited her in the hospital today," he continued. "She was just like always, perky and friendly."

"Why didn't you ask her what the hell she's up to?"

"I couldn't," he said. "I've never spoken to her of anything non-medical, and . . . well, I just couldn't. But I haven't been able to get this off my mind. I've been going in circles trying to figure it out," he said miserably. "The results of her surgery were beyond my expectations. And now I get served with these papers. The hospital administrators flew into a rage. They're considering a countersuit. But I . . ." His voice trailed off, hurt and perplexed.

I took a deep breath. I wanted so much to help, to give him an explanation. "Of course I'll contact her immediately and try to find out what's going on. But let me tell you, there's no understanding Helen. She's convinced you've saved her life; she tells everyone that. But it doesn't keep her from suing you. There's a big hole in her personality where a conscience belongs. I grew up with her. I've seen things like this before. All my life I've seen them. You can go mad trying to understand her."

"It makes no sense. But I had to talk to you." His voice sounded tired.

"It's unlikely I can influence her, but I'll certainly try."

I put down the phone and stood there, absorbing Helen's latest move. Then I went to my desk and picked up the letter from her delivered only this morning.

"July 28, 1971. Dear Kay, I'm still in the hospital, but not for much longer. It's easier to be here now that Tom is gone. (I can't believe it, seems like a bad dream.) I could always depend on him to help with whatever I needed. I don't look forward to being home, knowing he'll never come by. But don't worry about me. As long as Dr. Callahan's here, I have someone I can trust. I'm in good hands. Love, Helen. P.S. Do you realize it's been two years since the biopsy that diagnosed cancer? And one year since the first operation?"

Staring at the letter, I said aloud, "Helen, oh Helen . . ." I recalled the anguish I'd felt as a teen-ager when the full impact of Helen's personality confronted me. We were in such different worlds. My sense of responsibility had drawn me many times to try to understand her. But I lacked both the strength and the intuition.

In a high school biology class I had learned about General Beaumont, the surgeon. In the early 1800s he operated on an Indian fur trapper whose stomach had been perforated by the blast of a shotgun. In a flash of genius he decided not to close the wound with sutures, but to place in it a window through which he could study the digestive process. It was after that biology class that I dreamed I looked through a small square window in Helen's skull. I was shocked to see nothing. Her cranium was an empty chamber! On awaking I felt that now I knew why I often thought of her as a puppet with no internal control; why her clear blue eyes, whether sparkling in fun or wet with sadness, seemed vacant.

In school Helen was bright enough, but seemed not to be interested in anything. She took Home-Ec while Betty and I took Latin. She hung out with kids after school and came home late. As her infractions multiplied our anxious parents came to me with, "What have we done wrong?"

And I said, "It wouldn't matter what you did; she's in orbit beyond your influence."

My position in the family was secure: I was the trusted oldest child. If ever I was jealous of Helen it was when I'd see that nothing held her back from doing any outrageous thing she felt like doing. I was always afraid, afraid of disapproval, of being stupid, of being wrong. In an incident just before I graduated from high school Helen liberated me a degree. Dad was having one of his tantrums because Mother let us pick strawberries for pay for a farmer at the edge of town. This was demeaning, he said; people would think he couldn't support his family. When he raised his arm to smash the only good table lamp we owned, Helen grabbed a butcher knife. Holding it so tightly her hand trembled, she said, "Daddy, you son-of-a-bitch." Mother and Betty and I froze. We couldn't believe what we'd just seen and heard. The spirit seemed to leave Dad as he collapsed into a rocking chair. He sat there, chin in hands, eyes closed, and hours later was still there. I don't think he ever had another tantrum.

It wasn't until later, in medical school, that reading Cleckley's *Mask of Sanity* freed me from the burden of trying to understand. Helen was described on every page: shallow, labile affect; inability to learn from experience; anti-social behavior harming mainly oneself; intelligent, charming, outgoing, and amoral. Likely a genetic mutation and not amenable to treatment were the author's conclusions.

Labels and classification are requisites to medical training. The book's description of her personality enabled me to either ignore or tolerate her behavior without questioning or fretting about changing it. It wasn't until much later when her illness brought us together that I came to understand the limit of labels. It was only when I could see the matrix filling the spaces between the descriptive labels by which I'd defined her that I could appreciate Helen fully. And that was long after I'd separated myself from her in our girlhood.

Now as I laid her letter on the desk and pondered her malpractice suit against the young doctor she trusted, all I could see were the labels. Reaching for pen and stationery I began to write. "Dear Helen, I just had a phone call from Dr. Callahan . . ."

I stopped, pushed the paper away, and picked up the telephone. The nurses' station on the surgical ward answered. After identifying myself, I said in a no-nonsense voice, "Tell Helen I'll be down to see her at nine o'clock in the morning." Fortunately it would be Saturday. I fumed to myself for hours and hoped I wouldn't run down before I got to the hospital.

My heart was pounding as I took the elevator to the surgical floor. I'm sure I looked grim as I approached her bed. "Helen, what are you up to?"

She reacted with the big questioning eyes I'd seen before when she pretended innocence. Then I was even more angry.

"Doctor Callahan phoned me last night. I could hardly believe what he told me."

Helen fumbled for her notepad and threw up her hands as if to suggest that I wouldn't be open to her explanation.

"He was crushed by your legal action and of course extremely puzzled. I couldn't clarify a damned thing for him because the whole matter made absolutely no sense to me. You and I both know you couldn't have had better care than Dr. C. and this hospital have given you."

She fidgeted with her notepad and looked misunderstood as I continued.

"You know my feelings about unscrupulous lawyers. I can't but suspect an unprincipled lawyer has put you up to this." Taking a deep breath, I looked away from her and walked around the bed. I felt stymied. "Helen, how could you? Don't you know that you've destroyed the goodwill everyone felt for you?" I sat down on the end of her bed.

"Don't blame me," she wrote. "I only followed my attorney's advice. He said the legal investigator reviewed my medical records. The upshot was that I could get a bigger settlement by suing Dr. C. than by suing the first doctor for not operating when he should have. I didn't tell you because I knew you'd disapprove."

"You're damned right I disapprove. Who in his right mind wouldn't? You've sure been taken in by those shysters."

Anger and hurt poured from her eyes.

"Call a halt to the suit right now. Can I get your lawyer on the phone for you?"

She wrote, "Kay, you don't understand. I've never in my life had money. This is a chance."

It wasn't until several months later, when she visited Betty and me, that I heard about the lawsuit again. She was spending the afternoon with Betty; I was to pick her up before dinner. Betty phoned me that the arrangement had changed. "The kids got on her nerves, so she left to walk to a bar near here. She wasn't upset, just said she needed to relax where there wasn't so much noise. You can pick her up at Frank's Bar at Peach and Vine."

When I walked into the bar she was involved in animated conversation with the bartender. Legal papers were spread out on the counter between them. When she saw me she hurriedly folded them and stuffed them into her purse. I caught a glimpse of an envelope with her writing in large letters, "I'm suing for $2 million."

As her condition worsened, however, she seemed to lose interest in the lawsuit. She never again spoke of it to me. Hearing nothing of it again from anyone, I assumed she had dropped it.

– Chapter 16 –

The surgeon's knife, skillfully as it had been wielded to dissect away the invading tumor, did not arrest its advance. And the likelihood grew dimmer that the roll of skin peeled from her thigh and sustained for so long above her right breast would ever be grafted onto the gape in her neck. The doctors prescribed chemotherapy. "That stuff's poison," Helen wrote to me. "My blood and bone marrow can't take it."

For many weeks she didn't leave the hospital as one complication after another developed. Betty and I visited from time to time. We could see that the esteem in which she'd been held suffered a set-back as word of the lawsuit spread through the hospital. Her care was technically as excellent as before that imprudent action, but gone were the care-givers' love and admiration. Only cold professionalism remained.

Her letters were little more than accounts of her medical progress or, more often, the lack of it. Grim as her situation was, she wrote hopefully of what was to be tried next. "I'm going to get a new experimental drug, Bleomycin. The doctor says it probably won't make me sick like chemotherapy."

Two weeks later she wrote, "Neck's no better. Bleomycin didn't work. In fact, they thought it might be harming me. Don't know what they'll try next. More radiation is out. Might make the tissues break down even more.

"A new girl's in the next bed recovering from some kind of abdominal surgery and too sick to be good company. Already I can tell she's like all the others, thinks I'm deaf because I can't talk.

"Joanie, from the Derby, was here yesterday. She says Carlos (remember him from the Derby?) will take me home when I'm ready to go. Love, Helen."

Eventually she improved enough to leave the hospital. She would go to the clinic to have her dressing changed and to get supplies of bandages.

Early in the summer of '72 when I visited her I was shocked to find the tumor had made a bold leap to form a solid lump the size of an orange on the side of her neck. A few weeks later when she visited me its entire surface had ulcerated to expose a dirty yellow-gray base that oozed blood with the slightest touch—a marauding parasite in Helen's diminishing body.

Morning and night, she dressed her neck before the bathroom mirror, unrolling the soiled bandage and carefully lifting the layers of gauze from the gaping sore. Then meticulously, with the mirror guiding her, she'd place fresh squares of vaseline-impregnated gauze over the tumor and hold them in place with dry fluffs of gauze.

"Let me help," I'd offer as I could see that her arms were tired from reaching up.

She'd shake her head, smile thanks, and mouth that she just needed to rest a minute.

One morning, in spite of her precautions, the friable vessels dripped blood, soaking the towel on her shoulders and spilling onto her clothes. She dropped onto the toilet seat and sobbed as she pressed her palm against the seeping mass of cancer. I handed her fresh gauze, and watched, and felt helpless.

A few weeks earlier when intact skin had covered the tumor she had only to throw an attractive scarf around her neck to conceal it. But when the skin itself was devoured by the greedy invader the rotting tissue emitted a stench that kept her home-bound. Deodorants didn't conceal it and all the sticks and wicks and sprays did little but diminish the sickening odor of dead flesh. She no longer went out to shop, and she no longer made her daily appearance at the Derby. Several times a day she took a narcotic tablet. Swallowing was more difficult as the throat muscles became affected. Most of the time she wasn't hungry enough to make the effort to eat. Her kitchen was cluttered with cups of tea, bouillon and eggnog, tasted and left.

With her social activities so limited Helen decided to visit me again for a few days.

On that first evening, we relaxed listening to music and paging through the newspapers. I sat across the room from her and turned on a fan to waft the dead flesh odor outdoors. Helen looked especially tired and sad. When she began to write, I came and stood beside her to read, "You know, I've struggled against this thing for over three years and sometimes I just don't feel like going on."

I put an arm on her shoulder and said, "You've had so much courage for so long. I couldn't have done half as well."

Helen wiped the tears from her cheeks. "All those months in the hospital I was everyone's pet. The nurses marveled at how I never got discouraged. My doctor always brought the new residents to see me. I was his favorite patient."

"You're still loved and admired by everybody at the Derby, and they've known you for a long time. Same with Betty and me. And I love you more and more as I see your strength and optimism in coping with this cancer . . . Oh, I must tell you a dream I had the other night. You were a maiden, with sword and shield, on horseback, riding with other maidens at full speed along the crest of a hill. It was dusk and you were silhouetted against a fiery sunset. A Valkyrie maiden. It was dramatic and exciting, befitting you."

She seemed to be pleased with that picture of herself, then nodded sadly to indicate that it belonged to the past.

We sat in silence for a while, then slowly returned to the newspapers. It seemed impossible to me that at age 52 Helen's life was very nearly ended. Yet I never thought of how and when she would take leave of us. Instead, my mind searched for what else I might do for her. The remaining options were so few that I was beginning to despair.

I put down the unread newspaper and chanced the suggestion, "Why don't we visit the Reverend Plume down on the Peninsula?" I hurried to add, "He's not a conventional minister. He does psychic healing." The disbelief registered on Helen's face jolted me to recall how strongly our father's agnosticism had influenced us. I quickly assured her, "I found out about him from a parapsychologist at the university."

Slowly she looked up and gave a considered shrug of her shoulders.

"I know this takes you by surprise. Me, of all people, suggesting a psychic healer. But let me tell you how I arrived at this place."

She sat back in her chair, focused on what I had to say.

"My conversion, awakening, or whatever you want to call it, began last summer when Tony, a college student and my son's guitar teacher, came to visit me. He was more up-beat than usual.

"'I'm clairvoyant. I've taken a course,' he said.

"'In magic?' I asked. I was interested.

"'I'll demonstrate. I'll sit here,' he said, pulling a chair away from the dining table. 'When I tell you I'm ready you give me the name of someone you know and the age and residence.'

"Tony sat straight and still. He closed his eyes and took a few deep breaths. I waited. Finally he said, 'I'm ready'.

"I said, 'Helen, age fifty-two, San Jose.'"

As I described this scene Helen smiled and raised her hand in approval.

"Tony snapped his fingers and said, 'I see this woman before me. It's strange; there's a hole in her neck, right here.' And he pointed on himself to exactly where your tracheostomy is.

"He said, 'I see lines. I don't know what they are, maybe blood vessels, maybe scars, on the right side of the neck and upper chest.'

"Then he described the graft, the auburn color of your hair and your fair complexion until the source he had tapped into yielded no more information and he opened his eyes.

"My curiosity knew no bounds at that point. Tony told me how he had come by his clairvoyance, and two days later I signed up for the course."

Helen's eyes opened wide as a big question formed on her face.

"I discovered my own latent psychic abilities. I'd practice telepathic communication with my son and others. The point is not that I was somewhat successful, but that the experience brought a new dimension to my life. Here I was, rooted in science, suddenly in touch with a source of knowledge beyond the world I had known. The realization that there's something—some force, an intelligence—out there has altered my view of everything. Life has lost a lot of its urgency for me."

I restrained myself from telling Helen how, in the evenings, I often sent love and strength to her with all the psychic energy I could command. Nor did I tell her the joy I felt when she wrote from San Jose, "I've felt so close to you in the past few weeks. Sometimes at night it's as if you're right here in the room with me."

"That was a long way to tell you why I suggested visiting Mr. Plume's healing ministry."

Helen raised her eyebrows, looked from side to side, and extended her hands, palms up, to indicate she didn't know what to make of this. Then she looked long into the distance and seemed too tired to comment.

"Helen, I'm sorry I talked for so long. And said so much that you surely would never have expected to hear from me. Let's go to bed now. We can talk tomorrow about the healing."

The next day she asked me to take her home.

A letter a few days later said, "I saw the doctor today. He's a new one; I don't see Dr. C. anymore. I'm feeling kinda low tonight. He says there's absolutely nothing more they can do. They gave me a supply of bandages and some more pain pills. A visiting nurse will change the dressing. I watch TV and I have a lot of books to read.

"I was thinking about that psychic healer. If you want to drive down we could go to see him."

- Chapter 17 -

The next day, in the heat of early September, I drove to San Jose. We would go to the Redwood Chapel for a psychic healing that night.

Helen was waiting in her apartment, suitcase packed for a couple weeks' visit to my home. "I'll be glad to get out of this place. Haven't been outside for a week," she wrote. "But before we go I want to catch the six o'clock news—the Olympic shoot-out." She indicated the 12-inch TV screen on her dresser.

She turned to a blank sheet on the notepad. "The clinic has arranged home care for me. I like my housekeeper, a sharp little gal who can see what needs to be done. Last week . . ." she assumed an expression of disgust, "they sent a woman who couldn't speak English and couldn't read my notes."

After we watched the latest events in the Munich tragedy, Helen flipped off the TV and, pinching her nose between thumb and forefinger, asked with her eyes, "What do we do about it?"

"A few extra layers of gauze and a heavy spray of deodorant will probably smother the odor for a few hours until we get out of the chapel," I suggested.

Although I knew I couldn't match her meticulous way of applying each layer of gauze I offered to help her change the dressing. With every move I made, she twitched or frowned her displeasure.

I was accustomed to this. Even in the kitchen she took charge. She had little interest in eating, but she would oversee my cooking, adjusting the heat, turning the meat as if to rescue it from burning, taking over the white sauce with an implied, "Let's have no lumps."

When the dressing around her neck was completed to her satisfaction, Helen wrote, "It's dinner time, but I'm not hungry. Can't eat much anymore—only tea, broth, and Jello." Then, grimly she added, "I'm afraid I'm developing another complication. My tongue is becoming paralyzed. To swallow my pain pill I have to push it into the back of my mouth with my finger and then hurry water after it."

We agreed to forego dinner.

"Are these slacks all right to wear? Or would a dress look better? I don't wear dresses these days because my legs are so thin. But if you think . . ."

"Slacks are fine."

We left for Redwood City. The golden hills that stretched to the east of San Jose were grayed by summer smog. The air was oppressive. As we drove north I said, "The Midwest is green and lush this time of year."

"But I wouldn't go back to that summer steam bath," Helen countered in a note she held before me.

Nor would I choose to live again among the rolling hills and glacial lakes we had known as children. California had a hold on me. Not the California we viewed now from Highway 101 with its dust and heat and miles of little tract houses, but the California I could bring to life in my mind, from the Sierras through the Central Valley to the variable beauty of the coast. I knew the peaks from backpacking in the summer and skiing in the winter.

Helen wrote, "I've lived all over this state at one time or another."

"You started in LA during the war," I recalled. "After that we were out of touch. I probably don't know half the places you've lived."

As I drove, Helen wrote, "After Mac was killed on Okinawa I married John and lived in 'Frisco for awhile."

"I didn't know John except from Betty's letters and a snapshot. The fights you had with him scared the hell out of her. She was sure he'd kill you some day."

"He was a crazy son-of-a-bitch."

Although she had never seemed to tire of writing, now she let her pencil and pad fall into her lap as if in the moving car writing was more effort than she was equal to.

I said, "That snapshot of you in a Las Vegas bar is my favorite. John tall and handsome, you on a bar stool showing off your beautiful legs."

Helen looked reflective and sad. We drove for awhile in silence. Then she wrote, "I was a waitress in Long Barn for a couple of years."

"Long Barn?" I was surprised and pleased. "I didn't know you ever lived in the foothills. I used to go through there to ski; it's east of Sonora."

After another silence I added, "It was in the early fifties when you were married to Vic that I visited you in the Valley in that little stucco house at the crossroads. There was a tavern on the corner and nothing else in sight but fields of vegetables. The Army base was somewhere near, but I never saw it."

Helen nodded, a tinge of bitterness in her affirmation.

I recalled that visit in silence. I had just married my second husband, Jack. We were driving home to the Midwest from a visit to his parents in California. I had phoned Helen to say, "We're leaving from Monterey tomorrow morning, Sunday. Our route isn't far from where you live. If you're going to be home we'll stop."

"Fine," Helen said. "Come early, any time after 6:30. Vic gets home about then, I'm always up waiting for him. Have breakfast with us."

I took her at her word and we arrived at seven o'clock. Helen was up, expecting us. She looked great. "This is my husband Jack, a native Californian," I said. Jack greeted her with a shy smile. Then he retired to a corner chair and picked up *Life*, the only magazine in the room. Helen and I settled into catching up after years of separation.

"How many years has it been?" I wondered aloud.

"Since Mother went into the hospital in '43. I was in Nevada with John then. I came back for the funeral in '44 but didn't stay long. Remember?"

"Almost ten years!"

For almost an hour we chatted before I voiced what was bothering me, and what I was sure had been on Jack's mind ever since we arrived. "What are we having for breakfast? We were invited for breakfast, weren't we? And where's Vic?" I laughed to avoid sounding critical or impatient.

"Oh, I never keep food around the house. Vic'll bring something. He'll be along any minute." She went to the kitchen and returned with two beers.

"I'm not sure I can take this on an empty stomach, Helen." I'd never in my life drunk alcohol before breakfast.

Jack said a quiet no thanks.

For a moment Helen looked hurt. Then she brought some pretzels from a sparsely stocked cupboard. Jack and I had a day of driving ahead of us and had agreed not to stay long. After another half hour I said, "We really must go. Sorry we missed meeting Vic."

"Oh, you can't go without seeing Vic," Helen protested. "He's probably next door at the bar . . . But first, Kay," she added with a wink, "let me show you my new dress."

I followed her to the bedroom to see an expensive bluegray knit dress that made her eyes even bluer, and beside it a full length white knit coat and a golden brown suede leather jacket. "You have a talent for choosing the right clothes," I told her, edging toward the door. Surely, I thought, Jack's patience is wearing thin.

"C'mon to the bathroom a minute, honey," Helen beckoned.

As children the bathroom, and before that the outhouse, had been our favorite place for sharing secrets.

"What do you think it means that Vic's not interested in sex anymore?" she began abruptly. "Maybe I'm uneasy for no good reason. I don't think he's got another woman. But, hell, sex is what our marriage was all about."

"It's not a good omen," I agreed. "Why don't you ask him what it means?"

"Really, Kay, I don't even see enough of him to . . . Forget I mentioned it. Let's go to the bar."

The bar was crowded with men in cowboy boots and sombreros with their women and children on this Sunday morning. Vic was not among them.

Jack agreed to a drink but only with the promise of breakfast as soon as we found Vic. I squeezed his hand and hoped he was up to this experience. I wasn't sure I was. But we were 2000 miles from home, and perhaps ready for risks we would have resisted in Wisconsin.

"Vic'll be along any minute. Let's have a drink while we wait," Helen suggested.

"Helen, I'm reeling with that beer. What kind of a drink is there that won't do me in?"

"A stinger on the rocks, honey," she answered with flippant authority.

We had left Monterey about five o'clock on this morning. Already the day was making no sense. Now we stood among this roomful of friendly strangers, Jack and I with a stinger, that smooth mixture of brandy and creme-de-menthe. And then another, and another. Jack lost his shyness: he was giggling and talking to everyone who'd listen. Helen seemed to know all of them and their children. I clung to her to keep my balance as she chatted first with one, then with another. Finally, at a time I couldn't estimate, Vic joined us and I made out, as through frosted glass, a husky good-looking fellow in an Army uniform. We managed to wrest the bacon and eggs from him and, hanging onto each other, escaped to the house to make breakfast.

"We'll be right along, honey, after one more drink," Helen called after us.

As soon as we felt the relief of food in our stomachs, we collapsed onto a couch and fell asleep. Sometime in the darkness of night we awoke, piled out of bed, and groped our way to the car to resume the trip home.

Helen reached her notepad to me. "When Vic divorced me for the little Japanese girl, I didn't sit around and mope. I went straight to the Crossroads Tavern and found Tom, the best-looking fellow I'd ever seen at that bar and, to this day, the best man I've ever had."

- Chapter 18 -

THE FREEWAY OFF-RAMP SIGN ANNOUNCED REDWOOD CITY. Following the directions I had marked on a map, we found the Healing Ministry in an older part of the business district among a complex of small shops. People had gathered on the sidewalk in front of the building for the 7:30 P.M. service.

A young woman in a long full skirt the color of the setting sun approached us smiling. "I haven't seen you here before."

"It's our first time," I said as Helen nodded and pointed to her neck.

"Mr. Plume's the most talented psychic in the Bay Area. I come here often. Being in his presence has changed my life."

I nudged Helen and pointed to a sign in the window that described him as an "international psychic and, in smaller letters, "animal healings by appointment".

Our acquaintance confirmed that. "I've seen him accomplish miracles with animals, but his greatest gift is communicating with departed souls."

I was intrigued, but was reluctant to continue the conversation out of consideration for Helen. How was she reacting to all this? I had eased into an acceptance of psychic healing gradually over the past year. Which is not to say that I thought every claim of psychic healing credible. My acceptance was based on a good deal of scientific evidence, much of it acquired at a week-end symposium on paranormal phenomena at Stanford University only a few miles from here. Helen was plunged into this idea suddenly with little preparation except for what I'd told her that night of my encounter with the clairvoyant Tony.

The chapel doors opened and the twenty or so men and women moved out of the warm evening air into the small chapel. The odor of incense was overpowering. Helen sniffed and seemed about to register displeasure, then shifted to neutral. I knew incense only as something young people used to conceal the scent of marijuana. Perhaps it had a spiritual significance? I had a strong preference for unpolluted air; but tonight this heavily scented room might well absorb and conceal the offensive odor emanating from Helen's neck.

We sat in the back as far apart from others as possible, and had a full view of the room. I was overcome by a feeling of peacefulness. The chapel walls were hung with posters and paintings of psychedelic sunrises and flowers, stairs into eternity, and the traditional Christ. An altar, a vase of white lilies, and a fern were at the left front of the room; to the right was a small organ. A screen partly concealed an alcove behind the organ. I looked at Helen and our eyes met to acknowledge the uniqueness of this sanctuary.

A small white-haired woman in a flowered cotton dress and tennis shoes stepped from behind the screen and came toward the congregation. Her youthful face was radiant as she walked down the aisle greeting first one then another. She introduced herself to Helen, "I'm Mrs. Plume."

Helen wrote on her notepad, "I'm here for help with throat cancer."

"She's had the best of medical treatment but conventional therapy had been exhausted," I added.

Holding Helen's hands firmly in her own, Mrs. Plume said, "My husband is a channel for God's healing power. God has worked miracles through my husband. He's had this gift since he was a boy and has used it all his life to help others."

As Mrs. Plume moved on, Helen's hands remained poised for a moment in the space vacated by the hands that had held hers.

This emphasis on God worried me. I had omitted any reference to religion when I suggested to Helen that we come here. Psychic was the word I used. All her life Helen had denied a belief in God, and had often reacted with hostility to Betty's attempts to convince her of the benefit of prayer. Our agnostic father had influenced both Helen and me to reject religion. But now as I looked at her, Helen appeared softer, more yielding than I had ever seen her.

The Reverend Mr. Plume stepped from behind the screen. A small, gray-haired man in tan cotton slacks and a short-sleeved shirt, he glowed with the same joyful radiance I'd felt in his wife. His spiritual energy seemed to fill the room. A few years before I hadn't understood young peoples' talk of vibes. But vibrations were what I felt now. It was not the same room it had been when we first came in. I cast a questioning look at Helen and got no response. Her eyes were on Mr. Plume.

He asked a man in the front row to step up and sit on the stool before him. A few whispered words passed between them as the man pointed to his stomach. Mr. Plume said, "I know; I know." He shook out a tissue from a box and placed it against the man's solar plexus area. Then he made repeated boring motions with his index finger. A young woman, fair-skinned with a single long braid of blond hair, joined him. She looked as serene as Mr. and Mrs. Plume when she faced the man on the stool. At the completion of the healing she rose, placed her hands above the man's head and several times brought them down with a sweeping motion.

Others took their turns to receive God's healing energy. Between clients, and even during the healings, the minister carried on light conversation—the weather, baseball games—and was even jocular. His levity seemed to me incongruous with the gravity of Helen's cancer. He explained, "Once the flow of God's healing energy has started, no concentration is necessary to keep it flowing. I can talk and laugh without disturbing it. I don't have to be serious."

Helen's turn came. She walked, head held high, looking straight ahead, to the stool in the center of the healing area. At the minister's beckoning I moved to the front row. Immediately I was aware that the air about me seemed to be charged with electricity. Mr. Plume spoke to Helen in a low voice, then placed his hands on her upper back and appeared to be listening. All whispering ceased; the room became intensely still. Helen sat stately as a queen, only her neck bandage revealing her infirmity. The ivory pallor of her face above her pearly pink blouse suggested purity rather than illness. She was now, as I had seen her so often, the center of attention. The minister laid his hands on her neck as the young woman assistant held Helen's hands and signaled that the healing energy was coming through. They remained in this position for perhaps a minute. Then he moved away, took a card from his pocket, and wrote upon it. While he was writing, the assistant passed her hands in broad sweeps from Helen's head down over her shoulders and body. Mr. Plume read from the card, "Walk each day with God/ As onward up the path you plod/ He will enfold you in His arms/ So there is no need for alarm." He gave it to Helen.

With the card in her hand, Helen started back to her seat. In a surprise move the young woman in the long orange skirt stood up and hurried to embrace Helen, holding her own body firmly against Helen's afflicted side. Slowly murmurs and stirrings returned to the room.

We left as yet another person rose and walked to the healing area. I was filled with curiosity about Helen's reaction to this experience. But as we drove toward home her ever-ready notepad remained tucked in her purse. I felt unusually at peace and found it easy to withhold comment. If this had been a profound or spiritual experience for Helen almost anything I said might seem trivial or inappropriate. So, with her, I kept the silence. I would wait for her revelations.

- Chapter 19 -

"It's late—almost ten o'clock. Let's have something to eat. Remember, we didn't have any dinner before we went to Redwood City." I was hungry, and surprised and delighted when Helen nodded yes to food.

"Fish chowder? I made it this morning."

She raised her right hand, thumb and forefinger forming a circle.

"Why don't you get into more comfortable clothes before we eat? I put your suitcase on your bed."

She gestured that first she must change the neck dressing. "I know the smell bothers you," she mouthed.

True, the smell bothered me—a lot. But I joined her before the bathroom mirror to help. She unrolled the soiled bandage and tucked it into a plastic bag. With a saline solution in a bulb syringe she cleansed the cancer's raw surface. "How does it look?" she wrote. "The nurse told me to always check for maggots. Do you see any?"

It was not easy to inspect the pebbly surface of the oozing crater. I prayed that nothing would move. I saw only the now-familiar brownish pink surface reaching funnel-like from its rim at the skin to its apex undulating with the pulsations of the carotid artery. Reassured that no invaders had settled in, Helen began to encircle her neck with a length of fluffy gauze.

I went to the kitchen, and sprayed the air with citrus-scented deodorant. Then I put the chowder in a sauce pan to heat, and set the table.

As we ate, I sat across from Helen, expectantly. She had not yet commented on the "healing," and I was determined not to ask; I would wait until she was ready. She ate slowly and seemed to relish the chowder. There was none of the usual grimacing, or the use of a finger to move the food to the back of her throat. Food seemed to give her pleasure for the first time in months.

"It's good, isn't it?" I said.

Her eyes brightened.

At the end of our late dinner she got up, started toward the bedroom, and waved goodnight. She had not taken her Percodan tablet.

The next morning she looked rested. "Did you have a good night?"

"Slept the whole night without a pain pill," she wrote. As we sat at the breakfast table with tea and toast, she wrote, "Last night in the chapel—a strange experience." She shook her head. "When the minister's hands touched me I felt heat and electricity go through my body."

I said, "The front of the room was charged. I felt it the minute I went to that seat in the first row."

She smiled. I had felt a tinge of her own experience.

"But that girl in orange! When she put her arms around me my whole body was on fire."

"No wonder you look energetic today."

"I think I should go home tomorrow—if you can take me."

Surprised, I said, "Oh, not so soon. I thought you planned to stay for awhile. Of course, I'll be working; but only half-time and with flex hours. It'll work out for both of us."

Helen nodded agreement, and indicated on her fingers two or three more days.

Soon her sense of well-being waned. She rested more each

day and spent more hours in bed. A calm pervaded her that I had not seen before. In the evenings she sat in the living room with me. What was on her mind I could not guess. She wrote only such notes as, "Tomorrow I'll wash my tan sweater," or "I think I'll have my hair cut." She never made reference to her physical condition, to her increasing weakness. On the fifth day she held before me an almost full bottle of Percodan, and took one.

In those long evenings when I wondered what Helen was thinking, I thought about how my life had changed and what an arduous process it had been. Medical training had reinforced my ability to be an unemotional observer. During the first year in medical school I could cut off a frog's head and euthanize a dog, whose exposed heart I had just watched beat, with few qualms. My role models, besides my father, were male teachers and colleagues. It wasn't until shortly before Helen's cancer that I began to explore feelings, and venture into fuller relationships with people. About this time some of my colleagues were questioning the model of medical practice that addressed disease while keeping the patient in the background. I began to wonder, and to ask, how my patients' lives were, beyond the symptoms they presented to me. This led to fuzzy areas, hard to label, but it opened up ways to help. And it took me beyond the science of disease to the mystery of life.

Unlike me, Helen had seemed to bounce along on chance and whim, free of goals or guilt. She lived in the "here and now", not because of a guru's teachings, but because she was wired that way.

At other times, in the silence of our hours together, I found myself recalling incidents from the past that I really didn't want to think about.

In 1943, during the war, circumstances were different for both of us. I was in the process of divorcing my first husband. It had finally become clear to me that I needed a partner not a master. Helen, out of prison in southern California less than a year, did not contest her first husband, Mac's, divorce from her in

September. She returned home to Wisconsin from San Francisco that winter. But home no longer existed. Mother was in the hospital with congestive heart failure from which she would not recover. Dad managed alone and took a bus to visit her every other day. Betty lived with a university professor's family only a couple of miles away, where she worked for her room and board. So Helen stayed with me in a second floor flat that I occupied with my two small sons. I was a first year medical student living on an extremely tight budget and an equally limited time schedule. Every morning I got up early, made our breakfast, bundled the children off to the War Nursery, and caught a bus for an eight o'clock class. It was a stressful life, made more uncomfortable by the two elderly spinsters who were our landladies. They lived on the first floor, and kept a watchful eye on both the children and me.

When Helen first moved in we spent the week-end talking of what had happened in the years since we'd seen each other: her months in Los Angeles with Mac, her stint in the Women's Prison.

"Did Betty tell you about my introduction to lesbian sex?" Helen asked.

"Yes," I said, and stopped. Did I want to hear more?

Helen seemed to sense my reluctance. "Let's just say it was OK as a substitute."

I pictured myself like her, behind bars. I would be the outsider, restrained by conscience and fear from participating in forbidden pleasures.

"I can't imagine myself as a lesbian," I said. "On the other hand, men have been no great deal for me."

"Your life has changed a lot, from wife of a college teacher to this," Helen commented.

"The dean told me I had no business going to med school with two little kids. But they couldn't fill the slots with men because of the war. So here I am. Lucky." I got up and went to the kitchen to get an ashtray for Helen. "It's rough, though. A four-year course has been squeezed into three years because of the war. We're scheduled to be in class at eight o'clock on New Year's Day. Can't you just see half the students nodding off? We won't learn much that day."

"Sounds stupid to me," Helen said, lighting a cigarette.

"So what are your plans? You going to stay in Wisconsin for a while?" I asked.

"I can't decide. I'm at loose ends right now. I'd like to be able to stay with you while I figure things out."

"Sure, why not? I could use a little help in return. You could get dinner sometimes, baby-sit once in a while."

"It's a deal," she said.

But it wasn't the deal I'd naively expected.

Often when I left in the morning to take the children to the War Nursery, Helen had not yet come home. At the end of the day when I picked up my sons and came home for dinner, she had already left. When I discovered the ID tags of an Army Private under my double bed I knew how Helen spent her days.

I was alarmed, and angry. I couldn't risk being evicted from my apartment. I confronted Helen at 3 A.M. one morning when I heard the door creak open and then close. "You've got to find a job and a place of your own. You can't bring men up here. The old women downstairs don't miss a thing. It may already be too late."

She sputtered a weak denial before I thrust the GI tag under her nose. But nothing changed. Each night I put clean bed sheets on my bed. One evening I found a man's wrist watch on the floor at the head of my bed.

I left a note for Helen. In big letters on a sheet of typing paper I wrote, "NOTICE: This is no longer your home. Return your key to me, and find another place to live. Failure to comply will result in your eviction." I taped it onto the bedroom door.

The paper had been removed when I got home that night. And she was asleep—alone—in her bed. The chatter of the children awoke her. I hurried to ask, "Have you found a job yet?" When she sleepily mumbled, "I'm looking." I said, "I've had it, Helen. I'm giving you one day to get out." She turned over as if to go back to sleep.

The next night she came home to have dinner with us. As we ate she said nothing about leaving. I was silently sorting through what I might say: "Helen, this isn't fair. Leave before I have you put out, or before the old ladies have us all put out."

The next morning I discovered a ten dollar bill missing from the small amount of money in my purse. Enough to buy a week's groceries. My course was clear. I opened the phone directory to the first page and dialed the number of the city police department. Struggling to suppress the tremolo in my voice, I said, "My sister moved in with me a few weeks ago and she refuses to leave. I've told her repeatedly to get out. She won't. I've got two small kids, and she's disrupting our lives."

They picked Helen up at Mariotti's bar and charged her with vagrancy.

Belatedly, I shared my problem with Betty. She found a friend with fifty dollars to bail Helen out of jail.

Now, more than twenty-five years later, as we sat in my living room, Helen's only reference to those days was a note one evening, "I could've made a lot of money as a prostitute, but I always gave it away. Why was I such a fool?"

I laughed. "Maybe you'll play it smarter in your next life."

- Chapter 20 -

I STRUGGLED TO BE REALISTIC ABOUT HELEN, AND TO FACE UP TO her impending death. Heroic as physicians often are about saving life, we reach a point of acknowledging that nothing more can be done. Her physicians had reached that point but, as her sister, I had not. Helen's life had been far from exemplary, but she was only fifty-two-years old and much too young to die. I was not ready to let her go, not without one more attempt to stop the cancer's relentless advance. At this desperate stage in her illness it made sense to supplement the spiritual help she had received with anything else that held promise.

Laetrile, an extract of apricot pits, was banned in the United States. Both establishment medicine and government agencies had declared it worthless. Yet, in testimonial after testimonial, patients told of benefit from it, and the media generously reported their stories.

My own interest in Laetrile was strongly influenced by the experience of a friend, Pat, a social worker with a rare form of stomach cancer. When she completed the two months of chemotherapy recommended by her doctor, and mulled over the poor prognosis for her condition—only two to three more months of life—she decided to try Laetrile. Now, after taking the injections for about six weeks, she was eating well and gaining weight. Whether her improving health was a response to Laetrile, or to the earlier chemotherapy, or to an immunity response stimulated by her faith in Laetrile I couldn't judge. I knew only that what I saw was sufficient reason to obtain the substance for Helen.

Because Pat hadn't figured out how to penetrate the Bay Area's black market she had gone across the border into Tijuana, Mexico, to a large clinic that did a flourishing business in dispensing Laetrile. She agreed to get a supply for Helen on her next trip south.

Helen knew nothing of all this. How should I broach the subject with her? Again I would be suggesting something she might reasonably consider to be quackery. I arranged for Pat to visit us. A pale, slender, gray-haired woman in her early fifties, Pat extended a warm hand to Helen in greeting, and joined us in the living room.

"Kay tells me you and I are in the same situation: we've had all the treatment our doctors have to offer."

Helen nodded.

Pat continued, "I've been taking Laetrile for almost two months. I looked into it pretty thoroughly before I decided to take it. A nurse who's a friend gives me the injections. The main problem is that I have to go to Mexico to get it."

Helen shrugged and opened her eyes wide to suggest that she didn't know what to think of all this.

"I figure it this way," Pat said, shifting in her chair. "I feel better trying to help myself; that gives me hope."

Helen smiled, sympathetically I thought, and gestured good luck to Pat.

"Shall we give it a trial, Helen?" I asked. "Pat's going to Tijuana again tomorrow."

She mouthed, "I suppose."

I was disappointed by her lack of enthusiasm, but not dissuaded. I gave Pat a check to buy a two week supply of the extract.

Alone with Helen, I considered her apparent indifference. I had a sudden urge to scream into her ears that soon it would be too late, that now was the time to try what little therapy remained. I walked across the room and relaxed into a chair. I breathed deeply, and focused on Helen sitting in the recliner chair, pale and peaceful. I had been quick to criticize her skepticism. Now it occurred to me that her feelings might be more profound than I had realized. Perhaps she knew that the ebbing of her life could no longer be reversed.

The warm afternoon sun flooded the patio.

"Would you like to sit outside for awhile, Helen?" I asked.

She shook her head "No" and motioned toward her bedroom as she got up and walked slowly toward that darkened room.

Two days later Pat phoned. She had returned from Mexico without the Laetrile. The clinic had been crowded, the stocks were barely adequate for its own needs; none was available for patients in the United States. But she was not discouraged: she had obtained a password with which to contact a local source of the drug. She was confident that in a few days she would have enough medicine for both Helen and herself.

Helen seemed unperturbed by this news; I was frantic.

"Perhaps I should go home. You can let me know when it arrives," Helen said.

"But of course you can't go home," I protested. "In a day or so we'll have it."

Day after day, Pat scurried about within a fifty-mile radius of San Francisco looking for the Laetrile she had failed to find in Mexico.

Helen no longer talked of going home. She seemed more tired, and took less nourishment in spite of my pleading. Each day Pat phoned, related her non-productive wanderings about the Bay Area, and affirmed her confidence that tomorrow she would make the right connection.

Two weeks passed. It was late September, my favorite time of year. I felt autumn everywhere: in the hazy sunlight, the brown and yellow leaves that covered the grass, the sounds of children bickering and laughing at the school bus stop. Helen had always mimicked autumn in her choice of colors: in her auburn hair, her rust and coral suits, rich floral designs in fabrics, her brown accessories. This was her season, and the season of her birth.

I had continued to work half-time, although I was increasingly uneasy about leaving Helen alone. On this morning I decided to work in the yard for an hour before going to the clinic. The leaves and pine needles had blown into heavy patches over the lawn. First I tiptoed into Helen's room. "I'm going to be outside for awhile. Can I do anything for you before I go out?"

She stirred, motioned "No," and settled back into the blankets.

I went to the closet for a jacket, since it was cold in the mornings, and started to the back door. An imperative tapping from Helen's room stopped me in my steps. I rushed to her room. Blood was pouring from her mouth and nose, and rapidly covering everything about her. Stark fear was on her face as she jerked her dentures from her mouth and dropped them onto the rug. I pressed against the tumor on the side of her neck with one hand as I pushed with a wad of gauze on the inside of her mouth against the gushing stream. I pictured the large vessels in her neck ruptured by the eroding cancer, and I felt certain that she would bleed to death. As I envisioned her weakening, losing consciousness, and dying as I held her, a great tenderness filled me. I wanted this; I wanted for Helen to be finished with this terrible affliction.

Blood had soaked the bedding, the rug, and our clothes when miraculously the bleeding stopped. Helen raised her arm and pointed with incredible resolution to the telephone.

"Wait," I said, "I've got to keep the pressure on these blood vessels long enough to be sure they won't open up again. Then I'll call an ambulance."

I sat on the edge of her bed an interminably long time, trying not to move my hands, to keep a steady pressure on the rebellious core of cancer. Finally I eased away, and carefully adjusted pillows to keep her head elevated. She looked so pale and exhausted as she slumped against them.

I called an ambulance, then returned to Helen. With great caution I wiped the blood from her face, and then from her hands. I dared not remove the blood-soaked nightgown lest I disturb the precariously closed vessels. In the bathroom I dropped my own red, wet clothes to the floor, washed the color and odor from my skin, and pulled on slacks and sweatshirt.

I sat down beside Helen to wait for the ambulance.

- Chapter 21 -

her wrist. The steady rhythm of her heartbeat in the flow that coursed beneath my fingers calmed my own heart. The young attendant busied himself taking Helen's blood pressure, inflating the cuff around her upper arm, then slowly releasing it as he watched the dial. "It's pretty good," he tried to assure me. But I didn't feel assured. As visible and palpable as my surroundings were, this didn't seem real. I wanted to shake it out of my consciousness. It wasn't right for this drama to continue into the hospital. Not even if it were Helen's hospital, that new state-of-the-art facility where her condition was well understood, but especially not into my hospital, a crumbling county institution. I had been powerless to resist her directive, the strong thrust of her hand toward the telephone; and now we were fast approaching my hospital where she would challenge a new set of doctors.

To keep my misgivings at bay I concentrated on one thing after another in the ambulance: the oxygen canister, the mask, the defibrillator paddles, the cardiac monitor. Outside, the blurred images of oleanders in the mid strip of the freeway and of modern office buildings beyond affirmed that we were speeding toward our goal. I shifted my attention to the clothes I was wearing. How ridiculous I must look in these tight slacks and this faded blue sweat shirt. Why had I not put on something attractive? Gazing at Helen, I thought, my God, I'm preoccupied with my appearance while Helen is struggling to live.

I couldn't take my eyes off my sister. Her face was drained of color, her lips as pale as her skin. Remnants of the old bandage, blood-soaked and reeking of rotting flesh, still clung to her neck under the clean gauze I had wrapped over it. Streaks of dried blood remained on her chin, and blood matted her hair. The furrows between the tendons in her hands were deep where the soft tissue had wasted; blood had dried beneath her long tapered fingernails. I had never seen her look as thin as she looked at this moment under the blanket in the ambulance. That Helen should have reached this state of deterioration saddened me beyond description. Yet as she lay there with her eyes closed, an aura of dignity shone through the dissipation like a ray of light through an old shutter.

Then we were at the hospital. I paid the ambulance driver with MediCal stickers from Helen's purse. I gave the admitting desk the required information. And Helen managed to sign the authorization for care when the clerk steadied it before her. In a few minutes we were called into the Emergency Room. This was the moment I dreaded. I recognized the doctor, a cold dispassionate young man who, even in friendly conversation, was distant. He greeted me with a puzzled, "Doctor K., what brings you here?"

"Your new patient is my sister." I was sure he would have guessed the relationship if I had said nothing because, sick as Helen was, her resemblance to me was unmistakable.

He moved toward her with slow deliberate steps that lent profundity to his demeanor. Tilting his chin up as he looked down he allowed a studied frown to spread over his face.

I described the hemorrhage and briefly the background illness. If Helen had not been within earshot I would have added my understanding that little could be done for her medically. And I might have acknowledged that the precarious condition of the vessels in her neck would make examining her difficult.

"She's breathing normally," he observed. "With that much bleeding she'd have aspirated blood into her lungs. I'd expect her breathing to be labored."

He thought my account exaggerated?

He placed his stethoscope on her chest. "The sounds are normal, no rales at all."

I explained that nothing could enter her lungs except through the tracheostomy, the hole in her neck through which she had breathed for the last three years. I continued, "Surgery created a partition in the back of her throat so that the blood had to go to either her stomach or out her mouth. As I told you, a horrendous amount went out."

Several other physicians ambled over and stared impassively at the new patient. She gave them no clue as to her state of mind and little as to her state of consciousness. The only one who touched her was the nurse who took her pulse and blood pressure. I reminded myself that doctors who choose to work in emergency rooms want the excitement of torn flesh, broken bones, bodies riddled with bullets, and are not much interested in a middle-aged woman dying of cancer. Especially one to whom they could offer no medical relief.

The doctor broke the tense silence and, with an air of haughty boredom, said, "We'll send her down to the surgical ward and evaluate her after we get some blood tests."

An orderly wheeled her to Ward 4, to a bed by the window of a six-bed room. I cautioned him, and later the nurses, "Be careful when you move her; a slight jar of her neck might start another hemorrhage." No one acknowledged my advice. Unfortunately, I knew no doctors or nurses on the Surgery Service. My bailiwick was the Rehabilitation Ward where I had a good working relationship with everyone.

On this ward the nurses seemed uneasy around me, and certainly I was uneasy. The polarization between us had set in immediately. I didn't expect them to understand my anxiety; they had not witnessed Helen's bleeding. Besides that, my being a physician made the situation awkward, especially since I had no authority, no status on this service. I would have to accept being relegated to the role of a difficult meddlesome relative. But I was clear about one thing: I would not leave Helen's side. I must have conveyed my resolution because no one asked me to leave.

The nurses removed Helen's nightgown by cutting it down the front and peeling the upper part from her skin. Then they bathed her. Through all this they made no comment. I could imagine their disgruntlement at receiving a patient like this, a far cry from the clean surgical cases they were accustomed to. I desperately searched for words to break the tension, but my throat was as paralyzed as in a dream when one wants to scream for help and no sound comes. The odor from the cancer was overpowering. Why didn't anyone mention it? "Could we put a deodorant near the bed, for the sake of the other patients?" I asked.

The ward clerk came in and pronounced in a coldly efficient voice, "I'll need to take her watch and ring to the hospital safe." At that moment Helen opened her eyes and looked alarmed. For many years since Mac had given them to her, the gold ring with the solitary pearl had been on her finger and the dainty gold watch on her wrist.

"I'll take them," I told the nurse, as I assured Helen, "They'll be in my purse at all times, and I'll be here beside you."

Surely, I thought, on at least one shift there will be a pleasant compassionate nurse. I hadn't given up hope that the others, too, might soften and come to understand my concern and Helen's plight. The grim events of this morning flashed repeatedly before my eyes. I saw again the terror on Helen's face and I knew that I could not leave her to the routine care of others. If she hemorrhaged again there was no way she could call for help. If she managed in her desperation to find the call button, there was no assurance a nurse would hurry to her. And the curtains that hung between the beds for privacy would only serve to conceal her need for help.

That first day Helen was nearly motionless. When I spoke she opened her eyes but seemed not to see or to care. I offered her writing paper. "If you want to tell me anything, there's a tablet with a pencil tied to it here at the edge of your bed." I lifted her hand and touched it to the paper.

I offered her water. "Rinse your mouth gently," I urged, thinking how foul must be the lingering taste of old blood in her mouth.

I had phoned Betty late in the morning after we had settled into Ward 4. I was concerned about our sister's reaction to this latest development. Her denial of physical illness would be challenged now more than at any previous time.

Toward evening, Betty came to the hospital. She looked at Helen hesitantly, took her hand, and said, "It's Betty. I'm going to be with you for a couple hours."

Helen opened her eyes and feebly squeezed Betty's hand.

I had spared Betty a graphic description of our worst moments when I talked to her on the phone. And I would not burden her with them now. I was thankful for this chance to take a break and go home.

- **Chapter 22** -

As soon as I entered the house I went to Helen's room. The throw rug beside her bed was heavy with clotted blood. Islands of gauze and tissues dotted the glistening pool. I scooped the gelatinous mass into a plastic bag and then into the waste container for the next day's trash pick-up. The sheets, blankets, and rug I put through several washings in the machine. Fortunately, I had long ago ceased to be squeamish about blood. What bothered me now was to recall the episode of the blood-letting. How amazing that Helen had survived. When the evidence of this morning's calamity had been erased, I showered and changed into loose slacks and a sweater, clothes that would be comfortable for the long night. After a quick meal of leftovers I drove back to the hospital.

Betty seemed glad to see me, but made no comments, asked no questions. I imagined that in her characteristically secretive way she was trying to fit the progression of events into a cosmic scheme. She was also undoubtedly attempting to intercede with God on Helen's behalf. She was even more reluctant than I to concede to death.

"I hope you're up to another stint tomorrow. I'll need you," I told her as she eased out of the room.

That evening as I sat beside Helen it occurred to me that I should tell the Reverend and Mrs. Plume of her condition. Perhaps Betty's spiritual orientation made me seek a balance to my preoccupation in this crisis with the physical.

"Would you like for me to phone the Reverend Plume? There's a phone right outside in the hall."

Helen looked pleased and managed to say "Yes" with a slight nod of her head.

Returning from the phone, I reported, "I talked to Mrs. Plume. She said they'd 'send out' for help for you."

A slight smile softened Helen's face.

A little later she gestured something I couldn't understand. "You want a drink?" I held a glass with a straw to her lips. She squeezed her eyelids together and clamped her mouth shut.

"I'm sorry, honey, I just don't understand what you want." Then I remembered that she had not used the bed pan all day. When I took it from the bedside cabinet she nodded "Yes". When the cold metal touched her skin she winced and, with the first act of strength she had exhibited since coming to the hospital, she shoved it onto the floor with a bang that must have waked a lot of patients. I pressed the call button.

A nurse ran warm water over the pan and then placed it, I'm sure with more skill than I had, under Helen. She turned and left the room without a word. When Helen finished using the pan I again pressed the call button. When no one responded Helen squirmed and became more and more agitated. I pulled that bed pan from under her, covered it, and set it on the floor.

I had brought with me a volume of Anais Nin's diaries. Nine pages into the book Helen again wanted the bed pan. No nurse answered the call bell. Helen looked anxious and pointed to the pan on the floor.

I said, "Helen, it hasn't been emptied yet from the last time you used it. Try to wait for the nurse."

Half an hour later a nurse came and emptied the pan. When she began to slide the clean pan under Helen she found a dreadful mess of viscous black substance soaked into the bed linen and adhered tar-like to Helen's buttocks. She called for help. Ten minutes later Helen lay bathed between fresh sheets.

By now my worries about her hemorrhaging again were subsiding. She had done well with the moving necessary to her care: the bathing, the changing of bed linen and neck dressings. I settled into my book. But the night gave me no rest. Helen had developed diarrhea from the massive amount of blood she had swallowed. Most of the time I coped with her needs without help, struggling ineptly with bed pans and wash cloths. I had finally settled into sleep when the noisy arrival of the morning shift heralded the end of the night.

The next day, Helen's buttocks were flaming red, scalded by the residue of partly digested blood. She winced with pain whenever the tender skin was touched. On this day she lapsed often into deep sleep. Her respirations became alarmingly abnormal as they built gradually into a crescendo of ever deeper breaths, then ceased abruptly. I watched, wondering with each cycle if she would ever take another breath. But after each cessation her chest would move ever so slightly and her breathing would resume.

I talked to the doctor about her condition. When he told me that her hemoglobin, the oxygen-carrying pigment in the blood cells, was a third the normal level, the question of a transfusion naturally came up. It was his opinion that, in view of the poor prognosis, her life should not be prolonged by giving her blood. I couldn't tell him that I wanted Helen to live until Laetrile had a chance to help her. Meanwhile Helen gave us no clue as to whether she wanted her life to be prolonged. In fact, ever since she had directed me to call an ambulance, she had conveyed little beyond her pressing physical needs.

Again in the late afternoon Betty came and gave me an opportunity to go home for a couple of hours.

That evening I sat beside Helen's bed in tears. I was worn down by the many times I had imagined her to be dying that day. As I sat there with closed eyes I saw, as in a dream, two flat, reddish brown tiles standing on end with a layer of shimmering white sponge between them. Slowly the tiles were compressing the sponge until no air and moisture were left. At another time, I seemed to see a white envelop, with no message inside, covered with red dust.

Late that night a nurse came in and hung a bag of blood on the intravenous stand. "Doctor's orders," she said to my surprised expression. I fell asleep watching the drip, drip, drip of blood into Helen's vein.

On the next day, the third day that she and I had shared this corner of the six-bed room, color returned to Helen's face. She opened her eyes and looked around. She reached for the tablet and wrote, "Where are my teeth?"

"I didn't bring them." Before I could say more, a dread possibility occurred to me. I didn't remember seeing Helen's dentures when I cleaned the room. If they were in the red gelatinous lake on the floor, I had scooped them into the trash can. By now they were in the municipal dump.

"It's too early to put in your dentures. It's been only two days since you hemorrhaged." I hurried to add, "Your ring and watch are in my purse."

Helen seemed satisfied.

When Betty came to the hospital that afternoon I went home and, without much hope, searched Helen's room. The dentures were not there.

The phone rang as I was about to leave. It was Pat. "I've got a one-week supply of Laetrile."

"I hope it's not too late. Helen's in the hospital. It'll be hard to give her an injection there. But I'll find a way. I'll come by your place and pick it up in half an hour."

At the hospital the next morning a nurse came in and announced that Helen would be transferred upstairs to the Chronic Medical Service. This pleased me; it was an appropriate move. I assured Helen that it would be a change for the better.

There the atmosphere was vastly improved. The staff was oriented to the care of chronically ill and incurable patients. I didn't know her new doctor. But he was easy-going and approachable, and he had a reputation for being open to alternative therapies. It was such a relief to be able to talk to him that I confided my intention to give Helen Laetrile. He was skeptical, as was I. But we agreed that there was nothing to lose, and that it would be off the record.

Helen had improved enough to be aware of things she had not previously seemed to notice. After a few days on this ward she wrote me a note. "Dr. S. has a crush on you. I can tell by the way he looks at you." There was never any confirmation of this. But it pleased me that Helen's thinking went beyond herself.

My challenge now was to inject Laetrile without being detected by anyone. I filled the syringe at home, carefully packed it into my purse and, once beside Helen's bed, sneaked it out and quickly shot the illicit medicine into her thigh.

The next day, a sunny afternoon in early October, she asked to sit up on the edge of the bed. As I helped her I noticed a weakness in her left arm and leg so severe that she had to use her right hand to lift the left arm. She had had a stroke. A clot or a cluster of cancer cells from her neck had probably traveled to her brain. I said nothing. Nor did she acknowledge this new development. Sitting there she wrote on a tablet, "I'd like to put my stockings on so we could go out for a little walk."

Her desire, impossible to realize, to go for a little walk saddened me. We pulled on the stockings and struggled with preparations until she was so tired that she decided to rest and postpone the walk to another day.

I trusted the staff on this ward to care for Helen. I went back to work part-time. When she'd been in the hospital about two weeks, we began to make plans for her discharge. She would come to my home where a practical nurse would care for her when I was at work, and a home visiting nurse would check her and change the dressing daily. It would be difficult; but I preferred it to the alternative of a convalescent hospital either near me or in San Jose.

- **Chapter 23** -

Helen arrived home by ambulance midweek. What a contrast this trip was to the one four weeks earlier! When the attendants lifted her from the stretcher to the bed she thanked them with a wink and a nod. I didn't wait for her to acknowledge the bright pleasant room. "It's a big improvement from the hospital ward. Right? The sun pours in here from the east; it'll help you greet the day."

She looked about and smiled appreciation.

"A nurse's aide will be here with you when I'm at work. She'll start tomorrow."

Helen nodded approval. "And look at what I found in a stationer's store yesterday. This little bell. You barely have to touch it to make it clang." I demonstrated.

Helen wrote, then held the note pad for me to read, "I'm tired; I've been awake a long time."

Energetic as I had felt while I was getting her settled at home, I suddenly felt drained. After adjusting Helen's pillow and bed clothes I went into my bedroom and lay down. I realized then that throughout her long illness I had concerned myself mainly with the present, had not thought about what lay ahead. Now, with time running out, I dreaded to consider what these next weeks would bring.

I had decided to sleep on a cot in Helen's room, where I could quickly be at her side when she needed me. That first night, neither of us had much sleep. Helen was delighted with the bell. She rang it every half hour or so during the night and never seemed to want more than the assurance that I was there. After that night of testing and adjusting we settled into normal sleep. The fall rains came and the incessant soft patter on the roof eased slumber.

The nurse's aide was a kind, attentive woman whose children were grown. Before she arrived that first day I placed air-fresheners about the room to avoid her being discouraged before she started. She ministered conscientiously to Helen's every need: urging her to eat and drink, checking the urinary catheter, bathing her, and giving me an account of the day's happenings on my arrival home each afternoon.

In the evenings, after she left I prepared Laetrile to inject. Helen always cooperated when I told her, "Here's your shot. Hold still." But I was disappointed in getting no other response, no indication of whether she wanted me to continue giving her the medicine. As days passed without her improving I asked myself, "Why am I doing this?" Do I have an ego need to succeed where others have failed? No, I think the explanation is that I cannot bear to watch Helen die without doing something. And this just might help.

The rains continued without letup. I usually associated October rains with snow in the mountains and an early ski season, so no matter how depressingly dreary the rain, it was welcome. Not so this year when unrelenting gloom filled Helen's room and made impossible the cheeriness that I had strived for. I yearned for an end to the dismal darkness.

Helen lay for hours at a time uncomplaining, expressionless, Her left arm and leg heavy with paralysis. I often stood by her bed and wondered how she perceived her world. I had hung a picture on the wood-paneled wall near her bed, Matisse's Femme au Chapeau. An overhead light illuminated it and Helen could see it merely by opening her eyes without straining or turning.

She looked at it often and at times, I thought, quizzically. Perhaps she thought, as I did, that there was an aura of herself about it. The soft fine aristocratic features framed by a flash of red hair and a huge ornate hat, the bold splash of surrounding color accentuating the wistfulness of the small face.

"I got it for you when you were in the hospital. I thought you'd like it."

She answered with a decisive wink and a flick of her wrist.

Often, as I sat beside her in the quiet of her room, images from the past flashed before me. A scene that had always stayed with me, as clearly as if I had actually seen it, is of Helen, drink in hand, perched naked on a stool in her kitchen at midnight. Her partner is pulling on his shorts as they confront two policemen. She does not clutch for clothes to cover her nakedness. She glares at the officers and points imperiously to the door. "I expect the city to compensate me for that broken door."

One of the officers says, "We're responding to a report that you're cohabiting with a man you're not married to."

"Well, hot diggity," she says, crossing her legs, "I'll fuck whoever I want wherever I want. Now get the hell out of here."

This is the scene Helen described to me years ago when I was in graduate school and she lived near the campus. I don't recall how it ended; I remember only the daring, defiant naked girl.

Each day the home visiting nurse parked her little Volkswagen bug in the driveway, scrambled to open her umbrella, and dashed for the house. She was a pretty young woman, professional in manner. Helen liked her; she liked the clothes she wore, she liked the style of her blond hair, and above all she liked her competence. Her presence dispelled the gloom. On her arrival, Helen would come to life and reach for her pencil and pad. "I like that cute blouse you're wearing. I'd like one like it to go with my orange slacks." And many similar messages. I often thought that if I couldn't talk and if every day required more effort to reach for the pencil that I would restrict my writing to my most urgent, most significant thoughts. With Helen the more her body was consumed by illness, the more she expressed trivia, often in detail, including unnecessary pronouns and articles.

One afternoon as I returned home, the nurse rushed out of Helen's room to stop me. With latex gloves on and forceps in her hand she lowered her voice. "Brace yourself. I've just had an experience that I hope is my one in a lifetime."

"Oh, no," I said, adrenaline rising.

"I was changing Helen's dressing as usual. When I lifted the last layer of gauze I saw the entire raw surface was alive with maggots."

"Ugh. What did you do?"

"I felt sick. I wanted to just cover it up and walk away. But when I thought of Helen, and not of the maggots, I knew that I could do what I had to do. I called her doctor at the hospital. He said to spray it with DDT. So I went out and bought DDT; and the aide and I sprayed. Nothing is moving now, so we're doing a kind of mopping up operation, lifting out the dead ones with forceps. And would you believe it, Helen doesn't have any idea what we're doing."

"Can I help?" I asked, confident that she'd say no.

She brushed me aside. "I guess it's all part of being a nurse. But it's the hardest job I ever did. Tonight you may want to check and spray again if you find anything moving."

It would certainly be the last thing I would "want" to do. But, like the nurse, I could do what I had to. My stomach contracted with the thought of wriggling larvae. Nevertheless, I controlled myself and went into the room and stood by Helen on the opposite side of the bed where I could avoid seeing what the nurse had described. "Hi, Helen, I just want you to know I'm home." She opened her eyes sleepily and blinked.

That evening I inspected the open sore with a flashlight, found it quiet, and replaced the dressing. On the bed sheet near the pillow was a lone fat glistening larva. With my thumb and mid-finger I snapped it onto the floor, stepped on its bulging body, and recoiled with the burst.

That night as I lay in bed I was tormented with visions of a swarming mass of pink-white life that, but for DDT, would have metamorphosed into house flies. Why this last indignity?

Helen took less nourishment each day. I stopped injecting Laetrile. Even if the medicine could arrest the tumor's growth it could not counteract starvation, dehydration, and paralysis. In spite of the aide's kindly urging, Helen rejected all the food and drink offered her. In the evenings I made repeated trips from the kitchen to her bedside with chocolate milk, eggnog, cherry gelatin, all to no avail.

At other times I simply sat with her, book in hand and soft music on the radio. "What would you like?" I'd ask. She'd open her eyes and close them again. Her skin became taut over her bones as her tissues yielded up their moisture to keep her alive.

Once when she looked at me seemingly without pleading or understanding, those vacuous eyes reminded me of an unforgettable scene in a Brazilian travelogue. A herd of cattle was to be driven across a piranha-infested river. A lone cow was selected as a sacrifice to divert the fierce underwater marauders and allow the herd safe passage. The water reddened as she struggled and weakened under the murderous assault. The camera held in view her head with its empty uncomprehending eyes until it was sucked into the churning red of the river.

For the two weeks that Helen had been home with me the rains had not abated. While I inwardly cursed the weather she gave no indication that she was aware of it. She lived in pale pink nighties with ribbons and bows, lace and embroidery. An aura of beauty and purity enveloped her. Her pallor seemed ethereal, rather than of sickness. Betty came often to sit with her. And she seldom left without reminding me of the power of prayer to delay death and even to revive the dead.

Distressed, I'd say, "But why? It isn't right to want this to continue."

We were puzzled that Helen gave us no instructions, no advice. In the earliest days of her cancer she had told us, "I don't want you to spend money on my funeral. I've got that coming to me from the county welfare department." Now, only silence. Were there no messages for friends? No possessions to be disposed of in a special way? She gave us no clues. Her helplessness and resignation were almost complete.

Her face above the frills was daily more placid. Often as I watched I thought that life had left her, only to detect a slight movement of her chest as breathing resumed. In the week before her birthday, her friends at the Derby sent cards and flowers.

On October 20, the anniversary of her birth, the sky lifted and the rains ceased. Betty and I and the aide stayed close to her that day. We whispered to each other, not wanting to disturb her. "Helen, can you hear us? We're here with you." No response. Her breathing became more shallow, as the breaks between breaths lengthened. Then all movement ceased; her chest became still. At that moment sunshine flooded the room. Holding Betty's hand, I stood there filled with sadness and awe.

"She was a beautiful woman," the nurse's aide said.

- Epilogue -

Betty and I drove to San Jose to confer with Helen's friends at the Derby about a memorial service. As we walked in, Shortie was standing at the bar with a scrap of paper he'd pulled from his pocket and unfolded on the counter. "This is where he's supposed to be," he said, pointing to a spot on the hand-drawn map.

When he saw Betty and me, he explained, "Ted's prospecting for gold in the foothills near Sonora. I'm heading up there to find him."

"You're a fool," Bill, the bartender, cautioned. "There won't be much daylight left by the time you get there. Little chance you'll find him."

"Ted was mighty fond of Helen," Shortie said solemnly. "Somebody's got to tell him." With that he headed for his pick-up truck.

Neither Betty nor I remembered who Ted was, but that was beside the point. We settled down ("no drinks, thank you") and asked Bill and Joe and a few of the others what they'd like as a memorial service for Helen. We agreed on a mortuary chapel only a few blocks from the Derby at an early evening hour that would allow working folks to clean up and change clothes before walking to the chapel. The Reverend Mr. Plume would conduct the service. We knew that this was Helen's unexpressed wish.

When Betty and I arrived, the minister and his wife were the only persons in the chapel. I was struck by the appearance of the handsome, white-haired couple, he elegantly attired in a black suit, deep blue vest, and clerical collar, she in a simple black dress with a Navajo turquoise necklace. White braids framed her fair face and accentuated its serenity. The radiance of this couple transformed the red-carpeted chapel into a place of joyful expectation.

"There'll be only a small group of neighborhood friends," I told Mr. Plume. "Do you want any factual information about Helen for your talk?"

He smiled and said "No," in his crisp English accent.

There were three floral displays in the front of the room. A modest bouquet of red and white glads was from Betty's family. A bold arrangement of red glads and golden mums with a white ribbon lettered in sparkling blue was "from Friends at the Derby". Resting on a trellis was a large star of dozens of tiny mums sprayed a shimmering gold, and a card inscribed "Ted."

To the accompaniment of organ music, Helen's friends arrived. Solemn-faced working people, most of them were familiar to Betty and me from the times we had visited the Derby. When thirty or so had settled into the chapel's brown-cushioned seats Joanie motioned that probably no more would arrive.

The music faded. The minister stepped forward and, in a warm intimate tone, began, "We have gathered here in memory of our departed sister. I had not known Helen for long; I first met her about a month ago when she came to me for healing." He paused. "Now let me explain that I have been blessed by God with a psychic gift that I have used all my life to help others. Through this psychic power I knew that God did not intend for Helen to recover from her physical illness on this earth."

The congregation was spellbound.

He continued, "I did what I could to help her. I wrote this

message on a card for her to carry in her purse." He read from a small piece of paper he took from his pocket the message that Helen had carried with her in these last weeks. As he replaced the paper, he added, "And she was not alone; God eased her suffering."

Again he paused, took a few steps, and drew closer to the audience. "A few blocks from here is a place called the Derby."

Muffled laughter rose from the audience.

"You gather there for friendship and good feelings, enjoy a few drinks together. There are good vibrations in a neighborhood bar."

Smiles and nods of agreement passed through the assemblage.

"And that reminds me," he said with a wink, "of a Baptist minister's sermon to his congregation. He admonished them of the sinfulness of drinking and the evils of alcohol. 'The world would be a better place,' he concluded, 'if every last drop of booze was poured into the river . . . And now, my friends, let us sing *Shall We Gather at the River*?'"

Helen's friends were moved to subdued laughter.

Mr. Plume continued, "We are not gathered here in sorrow tonight. We are gathered to rejoice that Helen no longer suffers, that she is in her new home. I want to tell you that, through the power God has given me, I have been able to communicate with Helen since she passed from us.

"She is now on the other side undergoing adjustment and spiritual healing. Believe me, she is progressing well." He paused. "You should not be surprised if one day she pays you a visit at the Derby."

At that moment there was probably no doubt among those in the chapel that Helen, transformed, would one day return to the Derby.

Reluctantly Betty and I walked to the parking lot. It was not easy to accept that Helen was no longer with us. To ease the parting we were drawn back to the Derby. In the smoky dusk of the tavern, people who had just come from the service were milling about. Joe pulled us to the bar and ordered, "Two bourbons with soda for Helen's sisters." Then he recalled, "I used to walk her home when she'd had too much to drink. If no one was here to take her home, she'd call a cab to go that half block . . . We all loved her."

The Colonel, rosy-faced as always, joined us. "She'd breeze in here first thing in the morning and order a drink. Bill—he's the bartender—would say, 'Now we're officially open; the queen has arrived.' It didn't seem to bother her not being able to talk. She'd just wave an arm or point a finger and Bill'd know what she wanted." He paused and flicked the ash off his cigarette. "That woman was an inspiration to all of us."

"I remember the time," Joanie chimed in, "when some drunk hurt her feelings. She'd just gotten out of the hospital and had that tube coming out of her nose. This joker looked at her and said, 'Bet you couldn't pick up peanuts with that trunk.' Bill leaped toward him and pointed him to the door. Everybody was ready to jump that guy."

Carrie beckoned us to a table where she sat with her husband. "We've known Helen a good many years. She used to give up other things to babysit for us; she loved kids. When she got sick with the cancer, she never complained and never wanted sympathy. We worried about her when Tom died last year. He'd taken mighty good care of her. But she held up. She was a symbol of strength to all of us."

"Tom had a little bank account for her," Carrie's husband added. "She'd used up the money in it; I think she knew the end was near." He looked down at the unbuttoned top of his trousers. "I've put on twenty pounds since I last wore this suit. A lot of the fellows here haven't had a suit on for years until tonight."

"You all knew Helen pretty well," I said.

"She was," Joanie said, "to put it in a nutshell—alive, bigger than life. You could say she was a show-off—she loved attention—but it was never at anyone else's expense. She was upfront; always open with us about her condition. We knew about her treatments. When things weren't going well, she'd be low for a day or two, and then bounce back. She said, or did, whatever came to her mind, and we admired her for it."

Carrie's husband balanced the picture with, "But let's admit that she often did things that weren't in her interest. She was head-strong, and needed Tom to keep her in line."

"She was a flirt," Shortie put in. "She often came on as tough. But men saw through her bravado to the lovable woman she was."

All evening I'd been aware of Carlos, a darkly handsome man. He sat alone at a table, shirt collar open, hair falling onto his forehead, slumped over a drink. Carrie said, "He's taking Helen's passing pretty hard."

Joanie explained, "He used to drive Helen to the hospital. She took the bus for a long time. But after that day on the bus when she hemorrhaged from the cancer and couldn't stop the bleeding, she never rode the bus again. Carlos told her to call him anytime—day or night—and he'd see that she got to the hospital. It meant a lot to her that she could depend on him."

I went over and sat down at the table across from him. "Carlos, Helen didn't want to leave us. But it was her time to go. She knew it and accepted it." His reddened eyes looked for an instant into mine, then his head fell forward again. "Please," I said, reaching for his hand. "You were very important to Helen. But now you must let her go." I moved away from him slowly.

Betty and I left our barely-touched drinks on the bar and wandered through the room saying good-byes, shaking hands, embracing the folks we'd come to think of as our friends as well as Helen's. I knew then that, if Helen were to visit any earthly abode, it would be to mingle with those with whom she had shared drinks and camaraderie these many years.

KATHRYN SMICK has combined an active medical practice with family life and social activism. She has won awards for educational work on the dangers of nuclear weapons. Weekends often find her in the mountains backpacking or skiing. Before settling in Northern California, she spent her early years in Wisconsin.